BREWING BRITISH-STYLE
BEERS

BREWING BRITISH-STYLE
BEERS

More Than 100 Thirst-Quenching
Pub Recipes to Brew at Home

DAVE LINE

FOX CHAPEL
PUBLISHING

Dedication
To Sheila and Robert

Thanks
The concept of *Brewing British-Style Beers* (originally published as *Brewing Beers Like Those You Buy*) generated a tremendous enthusiasm from all those who knew about the project.

Space will not permit me to repeat and record my thanks individually to all the people who have helped. Even so, I would like to thank collectively the friends throughout Great Britain and indeed many parts of the world who sent information and samples of beers for analysis, which has enabled me to present such a balanced selection of beers for you to brew. Many of the regional draught beers were found at beer festivals organized by the Campaign for Real Ale, and I would like to thank the organizers and fellow members of the movement for their help and cooperation with the collection of these samples.

My particular thanks must, however, go to the commercial brewers and the brewing industry itself. Much of the recipe formulation was done from information freely given by the breweries who are proud to divulge the quality of their ingredients and practices.

Finally my thanks go to my wife Sheila for typing the manuscript and for her patience with my brewing activities and the chaos that reigned in our household during the writing of this book.

—Dave Line

Color illustrations by Mark Lockley.

Interior photography courtesy of Ewan Munro (*www.flickr.com/photos/55935853@N00*) and Nicholas Robertson (*www.breweryartists.co.uk*). Mr. Munro's images were used under the Creative Commons Attribution-ShareAlike 2.0 Generic (CC BY-SA-2.0) license. To learn more, visit *http://creativecommons.org/licenses.*

Special thanks to Avi Abrams of Dark Roasted Blend (*www.darkroastedblend.com*) for his assistance locating photos. Started in 2006, Dark Roasted Blend is an online magazine featuring unusual, innovative, and creative art, photography, and technology along with exceptional travel destinations. The highly visual format of the site gives visitors the feel of reading a large coffee table book. Dark Roasted Blend has been featured in publications like *Time*, *USA Today*, *Wired*, and *National Geographic* and averages 20,000 visitors each day.

ISBN 978-1-56523-689-9

Library of Congress Cataloging-in-Publication Data

Line, Dave.
 Brewing British-style beers : more than 100 thirst quenching pub recipes to brew at home / Dave Line.
    p. cm.
 Includes index.
 ISBN 978-1-56523-689-9 (pbk.)
 1. Beer. 2. Brewing--Amateurs' manuals. 3. Cookbooks. I. Title.
 TP577.L49 2012
 641.2'3--dc23
                            2011051147

To learn more about the other great books from Fox Chapel Publishing, or to find a retailer near you, call toll-free 800-457-9112 or visit us at *www.FoxChapelPublishing.com*.

Note to Authors: We are always looking for talented authors to write new books in our area of woodworking, design, and related crafts. Please send a brief letter describing your idea to Acquisition Editor, 1970 Broad Street, East Petersburg, PA 17520.

Printed in Indonesia
First printing

Because working with fermenting liquids and other materials inherently includes the risk of injury and damage, this book cannot guarantee that using the recipes in this book is safe for everyone. For this reason, this book is sold without warranties or guarantees of any kind, expressed or implied, and the publisher and the author disclaim any liability for any injuries, losses, or damages caused in any way by the content of this book or the reader's use of the ingredients needed to complete the recipes presented here. The publisher and the author urge all readers to thoroughly review each project and to understand the effects of all ingredients before starting any recipe.

Publisher's Note

The processes used for home brewing and home brewing equipment and ingredients improve each year. As a result, you may find some of the equipment or ingredients recommended in this book are no longer available or have more modernized alternatives. The publisher encourages every reader to visit his local home brewing supply shop for information on the best equipment and ingredients for today's home brewers.

About the Author

In a decade of brewing, Dave Line probably devised and had published more recipes for beer than anyone else in the world.

Through regular monthly articles in "Amateur Winemaker" magazine and his definitive first book, *The Big Book of Brewing*, he was acknowledged as one of the leading experts on home brewing in the United Kingdom.

People who wanted to brew the types of beers they drank at the local bar, but without the too familiar stigmas associated with home brew, have acclaimed his methods a major breakthrough in beer quality. He made it possible for the first time to brew commercial standard beer in the home using simple equipment.

Dave, who was 37 and lived in Southampton, died suddenly in 1979, leaving a widow and young son.

Table of Contents

Introduction

It took twenty years of brewing, experimenting, and drinking by enthusiastic amateurs to bring the craft of home brewing to the stage where we can produce beers to match the quality of our commercial counterparts. Given the ingredients and the methods, it is hardly surprising that amateur brewers will want to try to brew a drink like their favorite British beer. *Brewing British-Style Beers* sets out to help them in this quest.

This book does not explain how to brew exact copies of specific commercial beers, but rather how to brew beers that are similar to commercial versions. Using home brewing methods, it is impossible to turn out the exact same beer as a large brewery. What is possible is to emulate those beers with a fair degree of success. Similar flavor, strength, and color can be achieved and in such a way that you may end up liking the home brewed version better than the original.

I must clearly state that none of the recipes given in the book list (at least not intentionally) the exact brewing ingredients and procedures of the quoted beer. Although I have been entrusted with the complete formulation and brewing techniques for many beers, it would be pointless publishing them here. I have tried many times to brew commercial recipes, and in nearly every case, the brew turned out to be a disappointing imitation. To achieve the best results, it was often necessary to change the basic ingredients or even add others.

The limitations of home brewing equipment and availability of certain items have generally meant my formulations include more malt adjuncts and sweeteners. Home brewed beer tends to ferment more than commercial equivalents, giving a stronger, more alcoholic brew with a drier taste for the same starting ingredients. Home brewers cannot successfully filter out

PHOTO COURTESY OF EWAN MUNRO.

The Ship and Whale, Rotherhithe, London. Built in 1851, this pub's name reflects the seafaring history of the surrounding area.

the excess yeast or control the storage temperature to limit this prolonged fermentation. As a result, my brews may have different starting gravities and contain artificial sweeteners to help restore the balance in the finished beer.

Quoting brand names is the clearest way of identifying beer characteristics. Originally the book was just going to include a full selection of types and flavors of beers. My recipe for a "strong, full, malt-flavored bitter with a delicious well balanced hop bite" applied to Adnams Southwold Bitter, Eldridge Pope's Royal Oak and Gales H. S. B. for starters. And this was confusing because these beers have their subtle differences, and I know people who love two out of the three, but hate the other.

I cannot describe an identity for a particular beer any better than the breweries can themselves, so I have accepted the easy way out. If someone wants to brew a drink like Guinness, they know what they want and so do I. And this is what *Brewing British-Style Beers* is all about.

A Brief History of Pubs and Pub Signs

The origin of public houses or "pubs" can be traced back to the Roman Empire. In Rome, *tabernae*, or taverns, sold food and drink, such as wine, bread, cheese, and nuts. Patrons could also purchase and eat hot meals at these locations. Tavern owners often placed grapevine leaves outside their establishments to signify they sold wine. These traditional Roman taverns were brought to Britain when the Roman legion invaded the area. They were placed along the new roads built by the Romans and served as resting places for soldiers and other travelers. Since grapevines were not abundant in Britain's climate, tavern owners placed evergreen leaves outside their buildings.

During the crusades when pilgrimages were popular, taverns were built along pilgrimage routes to serve as overnight rest stops for religious travelers. Since the majority of Britain's population was illiterate, the tavern owners hung signs with images outside their establishments to advertise the building's name and purpose. During the crusades, religious images were popular, such as the ark, or renderings of various saints.

This tradition of "picture" signs has continued to the present day, and each sign's image has a particular meeting. A pub's sign could indicate the lord of the area, the predominant occupation of the town's residents, the type of entertainment available (cock fighting and bull and bear baiting), the country's current monarch, popular writers or political figures, legendary heroes, or even local villains. As time progressed, pub signs became a nod to advancements in technology, often featuring trains after the Industrial Revolution.

Take a look at this gallery of British pub signs and see if you can interpret the meaning of the images on each sign. The photos feature both old and more modern signs, but all include traditional and meaningful sign images. All the London photos presented in the gallery are courtesy of Ewan Munro (*www.flickr.com/photos/55935853@N00*) and the remainder courtesy of Nicholas Robertson (*www.breweryartists.co.uk*).

The Holly Bush, Hampstead, London. The image on this sign dates back to the time of Roman taverns in Britain. Because the grapevine leaves traditionally hung outside taverns to indicate the sale of wine were not common in Britain, tavern owners improvised, hanging evergreen leaves, like those found on holly bushes.

Red Lion, Upton Snodsbury, Worcester. The Red Lion is one of the most popular pub names in England. It is a symbol of Scotland and is featured on the Scottish flag. During the 1600s, England's Scottish King, James I, decreed that Scotland's red lion be depicted on the country's important buildings. Many tavern owners responded to the order by placing the lion on their signs.

The Cardinal, Westminster, London. Images of cardinals and other religious figures and symbols were popular during the time of the crusades. However, most pub owners removed or altered these images after King Henry VIII left the Catholic Church and established the Church of England. Pubs named "The Ark" often became "The Ship" and changed their signs accordingly.

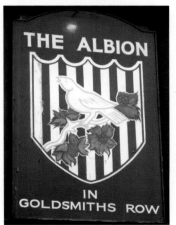

The Albion, Haggerston, London. Albion is purported to be the oldest name for Britain. Its etymology can be traced to words meaning "white" as well as "hill" or "mountain." Because of this, Albion is often said to be a reference to the white hills or cliffs of Dover—chalk formations surrounding the port town that would have been visible to approaching vessels.

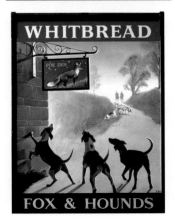

Fox & Hounds, Nailsworth, Gloucestershire. Pubs signs often honored English rulers by incorporating images of their favorite pastimes. King Henry VIII was a great sportsman and hunter. During his reign, many pub signs featured images of hound dogs, hunters, or birds in honor of the king's love of hunting and falconry. It is also typical for British pubs to be owned by breweries, which explains the name Whitbread at the top of this sign.

The Boleyn, Upton Park, London. There is no doubt this sign is a nod to the infamous Anne Boleyn, member of one of the most powerful English families during the Tudor reign and second wife of King Henry VIII. She was executed in 1536, found guilty of such charges as adultery, incest, and treason.

THE BOLEYN

The Charles Lamb, Islington, London. This sign honors English essayist and poet Charles Lamb. Many pub signs pay homage to English literary figures, such as William Shakespeare and Charles Dickens.

The Bricklayers Arms, West Norwood, London. Pub signs sometimes indicated the primary trade or occupation of the region, in this case bricklaying. Often pubs named for a specific occupation served as a meeting place for members of that trade.

Coach & Horses, Shipston-on-Stour, Warwickshire. When travel by coach became popular, roadside pubs and inns began to advertise accommodations for coaches and horses on their signs.

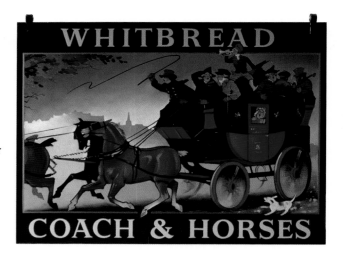

Railway, Caerphilly, South Wales. The advent of the Industrial Revolution and the steam engine brought many changes to England, including the arrival of trains and a railway system. Pubs were built along rail lines to serve as rest stops for travelers and often featured trains on their signs.

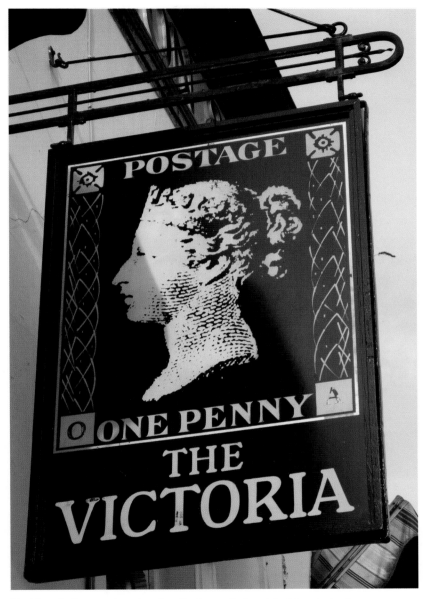

The Victoria, Bermondsey, London. The image featured on this pub sign is one of England's first postage stamps, containing the likeness of nineteenth-century monarch, Queen Victoria.

Getting Started

Home brewing is backed by a mature industry, with hundreds of retail outlets catering for our needs in equipment, ingredients, and literature on the subject. Because there is such a wealth of information about, I decided to make this book basically a collection of recipes, so you will not find a lot of brewing technicalities in the text—just sufficient to enable you to brew successfully. However, if after brewing some of these delicious beers you want to know some of the theory as to why they taste so good, then consult my first book, *The Big Book of Brewing*, which covers all aspects of home brewing. Do not forget, though, to raise your glass and toast your thanks to the commercial brewers who created the beers in the first place.

What is in beer?

- **Malt:** Gives flavor, strength, and aroma.
- **Hops:** Impart bitterness to balance the maltiness.
- **Sugar:** Gives strength and sweetness.
- **Adjuncts:** Other cereals sometimes used for economy and flavor.
- **Yeast:** Converts the sugar into alcohol and carbon dioxide gas.
- **Water:** Even strong beers contain 90% water.

Ingredients Needed

The list of ingredients used in brewing is quite incredible. Indeed, even the traditional malt, hops, and yeast can be processed, packaged, and presented in a form that can baffle a newcomer to brewing. Go into any large home brew supply shop and see the hundreds of different items covering ingredients and brewing aids—it's no wonder beginners get confused and embarrassed.

I intend to save you from experiencing these problems by briefly describing the ingredients used in this book and why they are used.

Pale malt grains. Beer is produced by the action of yeast on a sugary solution. Most of this sweet solution, called wort, is obtained by processing malted barley grains. Home brew shops stock these grains in a whole or crushed form. To be processed in the home they must be crushed and as the degree of crushing is critical, I would recommend not purchasing the grains whole. Crushed pale malt contains the light stone colored husks and the white powdery interiors. Pale malt represents the main weight of dry ingredients and cost in beer production and it is worth investing in a bulk purchase (say 100 lb. [45 kg]) arrangement with your home brew shop.

Lager malt grains. Lager malt looks very similar to pale malt and is used, surprise, surprise, for brewing lager! You need to get side-by-side samples to detect the lighter roasting of the lager malt. Looks are not everything, and lager malt is not a substitute for pale because different brewing techniques are required.

Roasted grains. Barley, whether raw or malted, can be roasted and burned to varying degrees to provide a useful means of coloring and flavoring beer. Only small quantities (½%–10%) of the total malt content are normally required. From a golden color to black, the range goes through crystal malt, amber malt, brown malt, chocolate malt, and roast barley to black malt. All these grains require crushing before use, but as the degree of crushing is not critical the grain can be purchased whole if desired and cracked at home in a coffee mill or grinder. If you have got to resort to thumping it with a mallet or chasing it with a rolling pin in your attempts to crush it at home, save yourself the effort and buy it already done.

Malt extract. The success of modern home brewing can be largely attributed to the availability of malt extract syrups. Although malt extract is a sticky, brown, cultured substance, it also presents the main beer ingredient as a very convenient manageable product that cuts down on brewing time, an important consideration for many following the hobby in their spare time. Basically, an extract is mashed out of barley malt and then the liquid is concentrated to about one tenth of its original volume. Also sold as a powder, in which case you will only need a small amount. Check the package label for more specific directions.

Barley syrup. Barley syrup is similar to malt extract and can be used as a direct substitute. Whereas the extract is produced by the traditional brewing practice of mashing, the barley syrup form achieves the required conversion of starch to usable sugars by other chemical processes.

Wheat malt. Wheat can be malted like barley but not with the same degree of success. Small quantities are used in the brew to assist the production of foam in the poured beer. A nice frothy head and a generous lacing of foam afterward is some drinkers' guide to quality. Brewing flour is this malt with the husks removed.

Flaked corn. Flaked corn is, and looks like, small yellow corn flakes like those found in some breakfast cereals. It is a cheap, easy to use malt substitute popular with English and American breweries. The corn flavor imparted is often the predominant characteristic of some beers.

22

Flaked rice. Just as effective as a cheap source of extract, flaked rice gives strength without color and is an ideal adjunct for delicately flavored lagers. It is readily available at most supermarkets, so you can easily pick it up during your weekly grocery shopping trip.

Flaked barley. Barley flakes improve the head retention, body, and flavor in beer. Dark beers can tolerate a higher proportion of this adjunct than light beers, which tend to remain cloudy through suspended protein matter.

Torrefied barley. Torrefied barley is barley where the grain has been enlarged like in many popular breakfast cereals. Make your own in a lidded pan, like popcorn.

Sugar. Commercial brewers rarely use pure white household sugar—it's too expensive and also it has had the entire desirable luscious flavoring substances refined out.

Combinations of invert and dark sugars, molasses, treacles and caramels are made up to suit each brewery's requirements. At our end of the trade these sugars are more expensive than the white, but don't be tempted to substitute for the latter because you will ruin the flavor balance of the beer.

Many beers are sweet or possess residual sweetness. For simplicity, I recommend using saccharin tablets, the type where one tablet has equivalent sweetness to one heaping teaspoon (5 ml) of white sugar. You can make your own invert sugar by boiling 2 lb. (1 kg) of white granulated (or brown if in the recipe) sugar in water with a heaping teaspoon of citric acid for a few minutes, then neutralizing the residual acid afterward. For the small gain in fermentation time it is not worth the bother. Much better is to buy brewing sugar (maltodextrin) from your home brew specialist, and use this in the same quantities. Lactose is a non-fermenting sugar used mainly for sweetening brown ales and sweet stouts.

Hops. Hop plants are perennial bines that grow twenty feet (6m) or more like giant green bean plants with left handed threads. Only the dried female flowers of the hop plants are used in brewing and these are best described as looking like reject Brussels sprouts. In the beer they impart a beautiful aroma, flavor, and bitterness to balance the body and sweetness of the malt. No wonder malt and hops are called the perfect partnership.

Many varieties of hops are available to the home brew trade and they have delightful names like Goldings, Fuggles, and Bullion.

Hop pellets are becoming popular in home brewing and can be substituted in all recipes with the recognition that they are concentrated and should be used in small quantities. The availability of some lesser-known types of hops is erratic in home brew circles and it may be necessary to find substitutes. For Bramling Cross and Whitbread Goldings Variety (W. G. V.), substitute Hallertauer.

Different varieties of hops are used to create diverse qualities of flavor
and bitterness in beer.

Isomerized hop extracts are concentrated, processed extracts of bittering resins from hops. They do not need to be boiled and can be added after the fermentation to adjust the bitterness level in the finished beer. The flavor is generally inferior to that achieved by traditional hopping techniques, so only small final adjustments are normally used to ensure a consistent product.

Water. Beer is nearly all water. So do not bother to impart this gem of knowledge to your bartender, because even if he appreciates that more than 90% of what he sells you is water you will not be thanked for ensuring all his customers know this fact as well!

For most purposes, water is a pretty inert substance—in its purest form a tasteless, colorless, neutral liquid. Water from the natural sources in rivers, wells, and public supply systems contains minute quantities of dissolved mineral salts, which can influence brewing processes to a marked degree. Chlorine is added to most public water supplies, and reacts with the hops to produce an unpleasant medicinal smell and taste. It is advisable to use a water filter or boil all water used for brewing for about ten minutes.

Most domestic water supplies are basically good brewing waters. The only problem waters are those that are hard, and this state is rarely serious. From experience the majority of people know whether water is hard or soft. If you believe your water is hard, then assume it contains chalk. Any doubt about it can easily be solved. Simply boil 5 quarts (4.5 liters) of water for a quarter of an hour and let it cool. Any chalk present will form a film or deposit on the pot's bottom. So now we have two categories for our water treatment: those with chalk and those without it.

Most home brew shops also stock proprietary ready-made water treatments for the different types of beer, which are perfectly satisfactory and an acceptable alternative to making your own as suggested on the following page.

Treatment for 25 quarts (24 Liters) of Water		
Type of Beer	**Chalky Water**	**Non Chalky Water**
Lager	1	—
Light Ale, Bitter, Pale Ale, Strong Ale, Barley Wine	1, 2	2
Brown Ale, Winter Ale, Mild Ale, Sweet Stout	1, 3	3
Irish Stout	—	4

Method

1 Add one heaping teaspoon of flaked calcium chloride or lactic acid solution, or boil water for a quarter of an hour and rack off the soft water for use when cool.

2 Add one heaping teaspoon of gypsum (calcium sulfate) and half a heaping teaspoon of magnesium sulfate.

3 Add half a heaping teaspoon of table salt (sodium chloride).

4 Add one heaping teaspoon of chalk (calcium carbonate).

Yeast. Yeast converts the sugary wort into an alcoholic solution by the process called fermentation, and in doing so gives off copious amounts of carbon dioxide gas. In the brewery, it is the behavior of the yeast that causes concern; in the bar it's the CO_2 gas! Yeast is a very unstable substance and needs careful attention in its natural wet state. Home brew yeasts are usually dried to give them better keeping qualities.

Fresh yeast from the brewery is best if you can get it. Understandably, not all breweries are willing to supply a sample although some are disappointed when you only want a cupful and not two or three cartloads of the liquid balm. We only need a small cupful to start off one of our brews. So long as it is sound, the yeast from one brew can be used to start the next one. Yeast reproduces about six times its volume during one fermentation so there is usually plenty to spare.

My second choice for a source of good yeast is from the beer itself. All naturally conditioned real ales contain yeast. One of the skills of the brewer and bartender is to ensure the beer served to you contains only minute amounts. So don't go into your bar and ask for a cloudy glass of your best bitter with plenty of muck floating about in it. You might not appreciate your bartender's sense of humor as he ceremoniously pours the treasured yeast brew over your head.

Seriously, 10 fl. oz. (300 ml) of yeasty beer is what you want. Yeast sediment from a quickly consumed cask can provide a satisfactory medium for starting a batch of home brew. It is best to come to some arrangement with your bartender so he can take a sample at his convenience and not when the bar is busy. Keg beers cannot be used because the amount of yeast collected is insufficient to ensure a healthy fermentation.

The recipes in this book refrain from listing a specific yeast strain to be used for each beer. This is because you can purchase hundreds of commercially cultivated strands of yeast through a home brew supplier or online, and there are often several varieties you can use to successfully produce the beer of your choice. When selecting yeast for a recipe, choose a variety that matches the style of beer you are trying to brew—use a stout yeast to brew a stout beer, etc. For more detail and guidance about yeast selection, visit your local home brew supplier. You can also check out the websites of these yeast manufacturers: Wyeast Laboratories, Inc., *www.wyeastlab.com* and White Labs, *www.whitelabs.com*.

Home brewing beer yeasts. These yeasts are usually dried and are sold in packets or tubs containing the coarse, light stone cultured granules. Yeast will only keep for about a week in the wet state. When dried, however, it can last for years and is ideal for home brewing. Unfortunately, because yeast is a living thing, it suffers somewhat in processing. I don't suppose we would take kindly to dehydration or freeze drying either, but anyway, what comes out isn't as good as what went in. A packet of dried yeast needs rehydrated in ⅔ cups of lukewarm water. Cover and leave for 15 minutes, then stir, before adding the yeast to the wort. For those of us who do not live near a brewery, and have not mastered the skill of starting with 10 fl. oz. (300 ml) of yeasty beer from the bar and ending up home with the same quantity, these dried yeasts are acceptable alternatives. I would recommend two packets of good brewing yeast plus a dose of yeast energizer (available from home brew suppliers) for a typical 25 quart (24 liter) brew. Although slow, the fermentation with dried yeasts is usually very persistent and continues past the normal stopping point at the quarter gravity figure. This continuing action results in a more alcoholic, less sweet and thinner bodied brew. Certain recipes call for the use of home brew beer yeast and these characteristics are catered for. However if you can only get home brew beer yeasts instead of the recommended commercial brewer's yeast, the flavor balance can be acceptably restored by adding five saccharin tablets. These tablets are in addition to any listed in the recipe. Barley wine recipes are not subjected to these additions, however.

Other Brewing Aids

Experience through the ages has shown the natural processes of brewing can be made more efficient and speeded up in some cases by the inclusion of other substances, for example, the mineral salts discussed previously for water treatment. These additions are now accepted as part of the technique for traditional brewing. Besides these water treatment minerals, we have the following aids:

Isinglass. Isinglass has been used in beer to assist the clarification process in the cask. In the dry state it has a fine white fluffy texture and when prepared for brewing by dissolving in acid it forms a thick viscous liquid like wallpaper paste. Actually, isinglass is the shredded stomach of the sturgeon fish and I often muse on what else was tried for clearing beer before this was found to be successful. Next time you find floaters in your beer make sure they are not swimming first. Nine times out of ten the minute whitish "breadcrumbs" sometimes found in glasses of real ale are only these isinglass finings—which are perfectly natural and safe. Just clench your teeth and strain it out. Isinglass tends to be a bit unstable for home brewing unless the temperature can be maintained below 64°F (18°C).

Gelatin. Gelatin is the home brewer's answer to the instability of isinglass. One half-ounce (15 gm) packet of gelatin made up to a solution with warm water and added to beer will clear a full batch star bright within hours. After learning that isinglass is processed fish stomach it is probably no shock to learn that gelatin is produced from calves' heels. But think, now you can boast about your beers having a real kick in them! Packets of gelatin are readily available at most grocery stores.

Irish moss. Outside the Emerald Isle, no one would really expect Irish moss to be a type of lichen. Quite logically Irish moss is seaweed. Commonly referred to as copper finings, the small pieces of dried dark green seaweed are added to the boiling wort in the pot, to hasten the hot break—the stage when the proteins coagulate and drop out of solution, leaving the murky wort clear. Incidentally, the dark green pieces of Irish moss can be purchased as a fine white powder, which just about sums up this strange additive.

Sodium metabisulfite. Sulfur dioxide, the gas liberated from burning sulfur, has been used for centuries to purify wooden casks for beer and wine. Please take my word for it that burning sulfur kills all known germs. Once I tried to cure some wild hops by setting alight some sulfur in the trashcan containing them. My colleague decided to check progress and lifted the lid, only to be engulfed in billowing clouds of choking gas. We had to abandon the house for three hours to let the fumes disperse!

The safer, modern approach is to wash the equipment in a solution of sodium or potassium metabisulfite. A 10% strength (2 oz. in 20 fl. oz. [100 gm in 1 liter]) contained in an empty liquid soap dispenser makes a handy stock solution. A two second squirt into another 20 fl. oz. (591 ml) of water makes a normal sterilizing strength ideal for purifying bottles, casks, siphon tubes, and other brewing equipment. Unlike a heavy duty cleaner and sterilizer, the wet dregs of metabisulfite solution retained by the drained equipment do not require further rinsing with water to remove traces since it is harmless in low concentrations. Indeed SO_2 is the only permitted preservative allowed in commercial beer. A few drops of neat stock solution keep beer bottles and casks sweet when empty. Do not use it in pressure barrels, as it will corrode any metal fittings in the cap, leading to unsafe and ineffective valves.

Equipment Required

Do not get carried away in your enthusiasm to brew some of these delicious beers and spend a fortune on home brew equipment. Using normal kitchen equipment and utensils, it is possible to brew and handle 25 quarts (24 liters) of beer for less than the price of a glass. Saucepans can be used to boil up the malt extract, hops, and any sugar that is needed. An empty semi-rigid polyethylene cube with tap, contained in a cardboard box, will handle the rest of the processes. These containers used to be very cheaply obtainable from stores and restaurants, but are now uncommon except from a few specialist suppliers. They proved very useful for resting the beer before kegging or bottling, and could be fitted with an airlock to protect the beer.

Although the technique works very well indeed, it is only suitable for the recipes based on malt extract. Even with these beers, you will probably want more finesse and want to consider the following equipment.

Some of the equipment needed to brew beer at home includes: an electric boiler, fermentation vessel, bottles, sterilizer, siphon, funnel, grain bags, bottle brushes, pots, yeast, a hydrometer, sieve, and bottle caps and a capping tool.

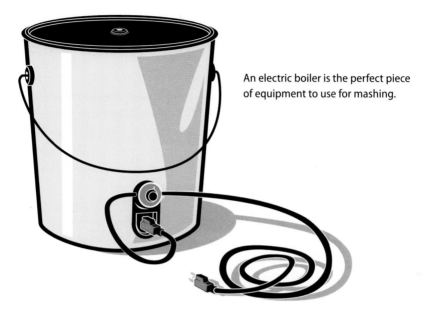

An electric boiler is the perfect piece of equipment to use for mashing.

Electric boiler. An electric boiler is a product custom built for home brewing. A typical electric boiler is a 25 quart (24 liter) polypropylene bucket and lid that has a pot type of heating element fitted in the sidewalls near the bottom. The element is controlled by a very sensitive thermostat and is capable of automatically keeping the temperature of the liquid or mash inside to within a few degrees of a selected setting. Since the thermostat can be set between 50°F and 212°F (10°C–100°C) it successfully copes with all the brewing processes of mashing, boiling and fermenting.

Fermenting vessel. Special white plastic fermenting buckets are available in home brew shops and in large chain stores. One with a capacity of around 25 quarts (24 liters) will cope with all recipes in this book. Ensure that it is supplied with a lid.

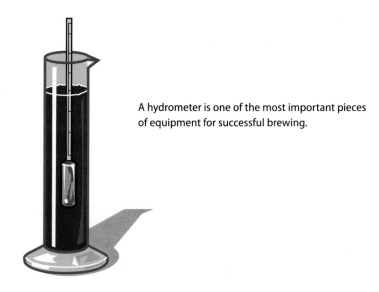

A hydrometer is one of the most important pieces of equipment for successful brewing.

Hydrometer. A brewing hydrometer is a graduated float used for measuring the amount of sugar in a solution. Various facts and figures can be determined from its readings from alcohol potential, the amount actually produced, the efficiency and progress of the fermentation.

Bottles. Only use genuine sound returnable glass beer bottles for your brews. Considerable gas pressure is built up inside the bottle due to secondary fermentation set in motion to give the beer sparkle. Soda bottles and the like, although they contain pressurized liquids, generally are not designed to withstand beer pressures. These days, most beer bottles are sealed with disposable metal crown caps. Rebottling with home brew will require replacement seals. Crown caps and plastic reseals are readily available. A special inexpensive capping tool is needed to fit crown caps.

Barrels. Take a trip to your local home brew supplier, and you will find a selection of pressure barrels made for the bulk storage of home brew, along with the CO_2 injection units used to keep the barrel pressure at the proper level.

Grain bag. Mashed grains can be awkward to handle, but contained in a grain bag are very easy to manage.

Mashing grain bags and insert bags for the electric boiler can be purchased in better home brew shops and are really essential for handling the mashed grain.

You can also make one yourself. The bag should have a capacity of about 20 quarts (19 liters). Its cross section can either be square or round depending on what shape the mash bucket is. For efficient extraction, the sidewalls need to be made from some strong, fairly impervious material, e.g. canvas, which can be used for the straps as well. Plastic diamond mesh (⅛ in. [3 mm]) as sold in gardening shops makes an ideal sieve for the bottom. Note that the grain bag holds more than 20 lbs. (9 kg) weight of hot wet grain and must be very well constructed.

33

Recommended basic equipment

- Electric boiler
- 30 quart (28 liter) plastic fermenting bucket with lid
- Hydrometer and jar
- Kitchen scales
- Large sieve
- Large saucepan
- Small funnel
- Kitchen spoons
- Siphon tubing

- Bottle brush
- 25 quarts (24 liters) worth of beer bottles or
- Large pressure barrel
- Thermometer (32–212°F [0–100°C])
- 5 five quart (4.5 liter) jars or a 25 quart (24 liter) fermenter fitted with an airlock
- Grain bag

CHAPTER 2

Enjoying Your Brewing

Let's get going and try your hand at brewing a batch of draft Fuller's Extra Special Bitter and then some bottled Guinness Extra Stout.

I have chosen these beers, which cover both malt extract and malted barley methods of brewing because they are beginner examples and will contain the fullest production details and explanations of why we are carrying out the various stages and what we hope to achieve. The thought behind these processes must be remembered for the main recipe section of the book, which will only lay down the basic instructions for making particular beers.

PHOTO COURTESY OF EWAN MUNRO.

Elderfield, Lower Clapton, London. This pub features four ales on tap, as well as a classic pub atmosphere.

Fuller's ESB

Fuller's ESB is one of the strongest draft beers in the United Kingdom and has a full malty flavor with a beautiful hop flavor rather than bitterness, rounded off by just the right degree of sweetness.

Our home brew version will be based on malt extract syrup and is an excellent example of how commercial type beer can be produced by simple procedures.

22.5 quarts	Alcohol 5.5%	22.5 liters
4 lb.	Diastatic malt extract	2000 gm
5 oz.	Crushed crystal malt	150 gm
2 lb.	Brown sugar	1000 gm
(2½ + ¼ + ¼) oz.	Goldings hops	(75 + 10 + 10) gm
½ oz.	Home brew beer yeast	15 gm
5	Saccharin tablets	5
1 tsp.	Irish moss	5 ml
1 tsp.	Gypsum	5 ml
½ oz.	Gelatin	15 gm
1 oz.	White sugar	30 gm

Method:

1. Boiling. Add the malt extract, crystal malt, gypsum and Irish moss to 15 quarts (14 liters) of hot water in the boiler or large pot. Stir thoroughly to dissolve the malt extract completely before applying more heat. The first quota (2½ oz./75 gm) of Goldings hops can now be mixed in and the heat applied. Boil for 35 minutes. The first 10 minutes of the boil will see the wort kick and froth up with alarming rapidity—so keep a watchful eye on progress. At the end of the boiling period, turn off the heat, leave the wort for a minute or so and then stir in the second quota of Goldings hops (¼ oz./10 gm).

2. Sterilize equipment. Meanwhile, clean and sterilize the intended fermenting bucket with a sterilizing solution used as directed.

3. Strain off. Using a large sieve or the grain bag, strain the wort through the mesh into the fermenting bucket. Wash out the remaining extract from the spent hops with a pot of hot water. The used hops can be discarded.

4. Add sugar. Dissolve the brown sugar and saccharin in some hot water and add this to the fermenting bucket as well. Add enough cold water to the wort to total 22.5 quarts (21 liters) mark with cold water.

5. Check specific gravity. When the wort temperature cools to 70°F (21°C), check the specific gravity with a hydrometer. The instrument is simply floated in the wort and the reading is taken at the liquid level. Hydrometers often have three scales, but the one we are interested in is marked with figures 0.990 to around 1.120 and denotes gravity. By some magic property, hydrometers always seem to stop spinning in the wort so that the scale you want to read faces the other way! Disregard the other scales on the instrument as these are used for winemaking; the information could confuse your thoughts in brewing. The specific gravity reading should be within a degree or two of 1.047. It is a good idea to start a recipe book and note all this process data as it can be invaluable for making any minor alterations to the recipe you feel are necessary to adjust the brewing equipment and ingredients nearer to your interpretation of the original brew.

6. Primary fermentation. Having noted the original gravity, the cooled wort is ready to receive the yeast. One packet of dried beer yeast can be rehydrated and added. In the initial stages, yeast requires plenty of oxygen from the air to assist the reproduction process. Using a sterilized plastic brewing paddle or spoon, aeration is best achieved by stirring from the bottom and lifting the wort and yeast to the surface. Replace the lid on the fermenting bucket and store the beer in a reasonably warm place with the minimum of temperature fluctuations. A constant temperature of 64°F (18°C) is ideal. Too low, the fermentation will be slow and the beer will develop yeast taints; too high, the brew may fall foul of sickly acid flavors.

Within a day, the surface of the brew should be covered with a light fluffy meringue-like topping of yeast. The crop will build up and sometimes form long protruding tentacles—quite a frightening sight the first time you see it. Also this initial yeast crop will purge the beer of unwanted hop fractions and protein debris. The dirty, brownish grey scum formed is best skimmed off the clean yeast.

37

Beneath the crop, the beer will appear to simmer through the vigorous liberation of carbon dioxide gas and the suspended yeast will give it a milky appearance. Certain strains of yeast tend to drop out of solution easily or congregate at the surface. These yeasts need stirring back in or rousing daily to ensure the fermentation progresses at a reasonable rate. Taking the hydrometer readings easily checks progress. Over the next two or three days, readings should progressively fall to around 10 (S.G.1010).

As fermentation abates the amount of carbon dioxide gas given off also decreases. Thus there is less gas to give the yeast buoyancy so the beer under the yeast pancake will start to clear. The primary fermentation has now produced the alcohol and the beer is ready for the next stage.

7. Secondary fermentation. The object of this intermediate stage of secondary fermentation is to remove the excess yeast and prepare the brew for its final casking.

The beer has got to be transferred to another vessel or vessels fitted with airlocks. Five individual 5 quart (4.5 liter) jars can be used, or a 25 quart (24 liter) fermenter fitted with an airlock. Clean and sterilize the 25 quart (24 liter) fermenter and add one heaping teaspoon (5 ml) of sugar. Replace lid.

8. Gelatin finings. Sprinkle the contents of one half-ounce (15 gm) packet of gelatin into a small saucepan of cold water. Let it stand for a few minutes to absorb and then apply gentle heat while stirring continuously. Completely dissolve the gelatin granules before the mixture boils. Add these finings to the empty fermenter.

9. Prepare for siphoning. Position the bucket full of beer on a table or shelf to give about 40 in. (about one meter) of head pressure above the fermenter. Place the hook end of the siphon tube in the beer and suck the other end of the tube to fill it with beer. Press this end to seal it and place it through the top of the fermenter. Release the pressure and allow the beer to flow. Keep the outlet end below the surface of the beer to minimize aeration. Transfer all the beer except the sediment. Stir the contents of the fermenter thoroughly, to disperse the gelatin finings. Replace the lid, or cap, and transfer the container to a cool place, around 55°F (13°C), but not lower than 45°F (7°C).

If you have a larger container for storing liquid, the beer can be stored in it, and in many cases, the container's tap can be prized out and the hole left is just the right size bore to fit a standard airlock bung. Alternatively, a bottle airlock system can be used as shown in the diagram on page 72. Actually since this particular brew will not completely fill the cube, the latter method is best. Before fitting the airlock add the final quota of hops. Dry hopping restores the hop aroma.

Now safe and sterile away from contact with air, the beer can be left indefinitely like this. In fact, three weeks is preferable, although since this is a beginner's exercise a week is adequate. I cannot have you dying of thirst while attempting your first brew up!

10. Fuller's ESB. The crystal clear brew can be racked into another container, and back into the washed container, taking care to leave the hops and sediment behind. Add the white sugar.

11. Stillage. The ideal place to keep the beer is within arm's reach of your favorite chair. Feet up, TV on, a full cask of beer and what more do you need? I keep protesting that the arrangement looks very attractive with the simulated wood effect cardboard casing, but mine always gets relegated to the cupboard under the stairs. I console myself that the cooler environment there is better for conditioning the beer.

12. Check pressure daily. Most sealed containers do not have an automatic safety valve to vent excess pressure. In the above procedure I have endeavored to ensure that there is only sufficient unfermented sugar in the beer just to condition it. The ullage space created by the under filled capacity will cope with the conditioning pressure. Extra hot days, though, may cause the cube to balloon slightly. Check the arrangement daily and vent any excessive pressure by drawing off a glass. I was going to say "and drink the beer," but it should not take long for you to realize these brewer's perks!

13. Keep air out. My early comments about beer in contact with air apply to drawing off glasses. Initially the conditioning pressure will ensure air is kept out, but when the cube is half empty or when a number of glasses are drawn off in quick succession, air could bubble in. On these occasions create and maintain external pressure by sliding and pressing down the palm of your hand on the top of the cube before opening the tap. Pressure barrels are much more reliable; they keep your beer under pressure and vent surplus gas automatically, and are far less likely to split or leak—always a danger with other containers that do not normally contain liquid under pressure.

14. Pressure barrels. This gorgeous bitter has been designed to be dispensed as real ale without external CO_2 pressure. But Fuller's ESB is often served with top pressure and if you prefer your beer this way then fit a CO_2 injector unit to the pressure barrel cap.

The filling technique is similar to the method described previously. Clear beer is siphoned from the secondary fermenter into the sterilized barrel and filled to leave a quart of ullage space. Add the white sugar. Prepare the gas injector unit. Close the control valve. Fit a new CO_2 cartridge and screw in the holder to puncture it. Screw the filler cap loosely on the barrel thread. Open the control valve for a second or two to let a burst of CO_2 gas into the ullage space. This action will purge out any air present. Screw the filler cap on tightly. The beer is now under pressure and can be drawn off.

Other CO_2 injector units regulate the pressure automatically or just inject CO_2 to push the beer out of the barrel. The latter types usually have a handle that acts as the control valve to let the gas in. Use these devices strictly as directed on the instructions.

Guinness Extra Stout

The final part of your brewing apprenticeship is to try your hand at brewing 25 quarts (24 liters) of Guinness, which, by my reckoning, is the best beer in the world.

As with the majority of beers in this book, Guinness is based on malted barley grains and this recipe demonstrates how to brew a typical grain beer. Differences in the common mashing methods will be highlighted.

25 quarts	Original Gravity 1.045	25 liters
7 lb.	Crushed pale malt	3500 gm
2 lb.	Flaked barley	1000 gm
1 lb.	Crushed roasted barley	500 gm
1 oz.	Bullion hops	30 gm
3 oz.	Northern Brewer hops	100 gm
	Yeast from Whitbread White Shield, or any other of the many bottle-conditioned beers now on sale	
	Temporary hard water (containing chalk)	

Brewing this stout takes some planning because you will be using the yeast from a bottle-conditioned beer. Four or five days before the main brewing session, take a trip down to your neglected bar and purchase a bottle. Try without exhausting your bartender's patience too much to select a bottle with a good ring of yeast clinging to the bottom. Ideally the bottles should be inspected under a strong light to assess the amount of yeast deposit. If there is any doubt, buy two or three bottles and drink the surplus beer. Although one bottle is usually sufficient to provide a good working starter in a few days, the purchasing additional bottles does give an excuse to savor some beer.

41

The yeast lifted from a bottle of Guinness was the best I have come across for home brewing top fermented English beers, but for many years, Guinness has been pasteurized.

Method:

1. Make a yeast starter. It is worth taking extra care with the cultivation of a good yeast sample. Yeast performance and characteristics vary with the gravity and nutrient properties of the wort and can be ruined by an alien environment. Bearing this in mind I like to make up my starter to emulate a Guinness wort. A 13.5 fl. oz. (400 ml) starter consisting of the bottom third of the bottle-conditioned beer topped up with a mixture of two tablespoons (50 gm) of malt extract syrup in water should do the trick.

The day before brewing, the yeast in the starter bottle should be working vigorously. Do not start the brewing session unless you are confident the yeast is strong enough to finish the job.

2. Mashing. There are three distinct techniques for mashing at home and I will describe examples for each method. Which one you choose depends largely on how much you can afford. The more you spend, the less effort you employ.

Mashing using a large pot/pan

Method 1: Large boiling pan

As many home brewers already possess a boiler of some sort for their beer making, it is likely this piece of essential equipment will double as a mash bucket as well. To cater for the largest brews requiring up to 10 lb. (4.5 kg) of dry grain, the boiler, pot, or large boiling pan used should not be smaller than a 22.5 quart (21 liter) capacity

The dry grains and cereals need to be mixed with hot water to form a smooth porridge To achieve the correct mix of grist (includes all crushed malt grains, roast malts, flaked and flavored cereals) to water, use the following ratios:

FOR MASHING:
- Mix 1 lb. of grist with 50–60 fl. oz. of water
- or 1 kg of grist with 3.2–3.75 liters of water.

For our Guinness brew, the grist totals 7 lb. (3500 gm) of malt, 2 lb. (1000 gm) of flaked barley and 1 lb. (500 gm) of roast barley, for a total of 10 lb. of grain. From the previous guidelines, ideally, 20 quarts (19 liters) of water are required for mashing, although 15 quarts (14 liters) can be tolerated with limited mashing capacity.

Pour the water and water treatment salts into the pan. Apply heat and raise the temperature up to 140°F (60°C). Gradually stir in the dry grist to form a smooth mixture. Keep stirring and slowly raise the temperature of the mix to 153°F (67°C). Turn off the heat and let the mash stand for 1½ hours. It will be necessary to reheat the mash back to the temperature 149°–153°F (65°–67°C) a couple of times as it cools. When applying heat during any mashing technique, constant stirring is essential to prevent hot spots prematurely killing off the enzymes that do the starch conversion.

Method 2: Electric boiler

As in method 1, use 20 quarts (19 liters) of water and follow the method 1 procedure for the initial mixing and raising to 153°F (67°C). Afterward, adjust the dial setting to keep the mash temperature between 144–151°F (62–66°C).

43

This setting can be identified by finding the dial setting that makes the thermostat click on and off. From then the process needs no further attention except for an occasional stir.

Method 3: Floating Mash Tun

Brewers with large (50 quart [47 liter]) boilers can often enjoy the convenience of the floating mash tun system. Half fill the boiler and raise the water temperature to 167°F (75°C). Pour the dry grist into a grain bag lining a large bucket fitted with a tap and lid. Mix the grain with enough of the boiler water

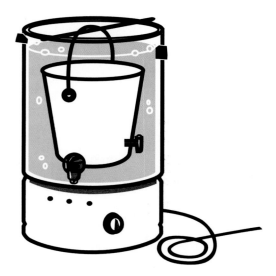

Sparging helps ensure that flavor from the hops and grains becomes a part of the wort.

to form a thick mix. The temperature of the resultant mix should be around 151°F (66°C). Replace the bucket lid and float the mash tun in the remaining boiler water for 1½ hours to complete the mashing. After saccharification, the boiler water can be removed and used to rinse the extract from the mashed grain back into the boiler for the boil with the hops.

3. Sparging your wort. It is worth starting home brewing just to have this exhilarating experience—what other hobby can offer such a wealth of verbal expressions? Telling people you have been sparging your wort initiates some incredible responses from blank disbelief to utter disgust!

Actually it's the retrieval of the rich malt sugars from the mashed grain. And it is a very necessary stage in our brewing.

Depending on the mashing method you adopted, the mashed grain may or may not be already contained in the grain bag. If it is not, as would be the case with the boiler methods, the hot grain must be transferred to the grain bag. First of all the bag must be supported or contained some way so that the wort can be run off into another receiver or direct into the boiler. Obviously the floating mash tun bucket satisfies this requirement already. I made a simple wort tray using a cut off section from a polyethylene cube for using after mashing in my electric boiler. Alternatively the bag can be supported in a bucket with a tap.

The rich wort will start draining off immediately but will be rather cloudy and hence it is best to collect the first jug or so and return it to the surface of the grain before letting the rest flow into the boiler. Let the grains drain naturally until reasonably dry then gently pour hot water (around 158°F [70°C]) over the grain surface. Continue this sparging with more hot water until 20 quarts (19 liters) of wort are collected.

4. Boiling. Boil the wort with all the hops for one hour. Strain the wort off the hops into a fermenting bucket and top up to the final quantity with cold water.

5. Brewing efficiency. When cool, the 25 quarts (24 liters) of wort should float a specific gravity between 1.045 and 1.053. In designing this recipe I purposely erred on the strong side so a beginner to mashing could, even with an inefficient extraction, still brew a stout with the strength of Guinness. The high figure of 1.053 is what a commercial brewery would be likely to achieve with sophisticated plant. Using my mashing methods, you should achieve an original gravity of 1.045 quite easily.

6. Fermentation. Getting back to the brewing, the cooled wort is now ready to receive the yeast. Add the starter bottle contents and aerate the wort for a minute or two. Replace the bucket lid and ferment the wort in a warm place. After three or four days, when the specific gravity has fallen to around 1.012, rack the beer into a sterilized container fitted with an airlock. Let the stout stand in this vessel for another week to fall bright naturally.

7. Bottling. Collect 25 quarts (24 liters) worth of beer bottles. Never use the fragile one-trip disposable bottles. Inspect them to ensure they are mechanically sound; no chips, cracks etc., and give them a thorough cleaning using a sterilizing powder. Afterward, give the bottles a good rinse out with cold water. Alternatively, a bit of hard work with hot water and a bottle brush will satisfy the cleaning requirements, although the bottles need sterilizing to ensure purity.

47

8. Sterilizing bottles. Add a generous squirt of 10% sodium metabisulfite solution to 20 fl. oz. (591 ml) of hot water and funnel the mix from one bottle to another. Drain thoroughly, but do not bother to rinse.

9. Priming. The stout at this stage retains very little carbon dioxide gas and is flat. To promote condition and more gas in the bottle, the fermentation process must be rekindled. Line up the bottles and funnel into each one a dose of white sugar at the rate of half a heaping teaspoon per 20 fl. oz. of capacity (5 ml per liter). Alternatively, stir into the bulk beer, 2½ oz. (75 g) of sugar dissolved in a little hot water.

10. Filling. Position the container of stout on a table or shelf and line up the bottles on the floor below. Useful accessories are an empty beer glass and a mopping up cloth. The glass is to have crafty sippers to check that it is all right (very essential) and the cloth to soak up any spillages that might and usually do occur.

Siphon the beer into the bottles. Keep the end of the tube near the bottle bottom to avoid frothing. It is essential that the bottles are not completely filled. Leave a minimum air space of ¾ in. per 20 fl. oz. or 40 mm per liter bottle. The airspace above the beer acts as a safety reservoir to contain the excess gas given off by the bottle fermentation.

Fit the bottle seals as appropriate.

11. Maturation. Guinness requires seven to ten day maturation in the bottle stored in a reasonably warm place before transferring the bottles to a cool storage place. Start drinking the ale after this time to check its condition. Like the real thing, our stout is best consumed within a month, which is rarely a problem for thirsty home brewers.

Variation: Draft Guinness

Draft Guinness is one of few examples where modern technology has benefitted a beer from the drinker's point of view. In a keg process, Guinness is injected mainly with nitrogen gas instead of the usual carbon dioxide. Nitrogen promotes a much smoother flavor and a fine creamy head. I have injected my home brew version with nitrogen gas with a remarkable degree of success, but the system is out of the scope of most home brewers. Using a measure of heading liquid or powder and dispensing the stout under pressure from a barrel is an acceptable compromise. Draft Guinness is approximately 80% of strength of the bottled version with original gravity around 1.038. Use the same ratio of ingredients, but cut down by one-fifth for the draft version. Alternatively, dilute the 25 quart (24 liter) brew up to 31.25 quarts (30 liters), but somehow I just cannot bring myself to do this. Adding water to this excellent ale seems sacrilege.

Bottled Beers

You are now ready to tackle brewing any of the hundred or so beers in the chapters that follow. Only the basic facts about the brewing ingredients and method required will be given.

There are four columns of information regarding the ingredients. The main list is the ingredients itself and is flanked by both U.S. and metric quantities. Do not, however, cross-reference the two weight systems, as the final volumes of beer will not be the same, i.e. 25 quarts is not equivalent to 25 liters and the ingredients list reflects this difference.

The first column on the left hand side gives a Stage number reference for each ingredient. This number refers to the Brewing Stage at which this particular ingredient is used. Certain ingredients have the weight subdivided as in the Brown Jack Best Brown Ale recipe (see page 51) where the roast barley is listed as (2½ + ½) oz. with corresponding Stage references of 1 and 2. This means that 2½ oz. are used in brewing Stage 1 and ½ oz. is used later in Stage 2.

Another point to clarify on the ingredients list is regarding the concentrated hop extracts. Sometimes these are sold in tubs marked "Sufficient for 20 quarts (19 liters)." In these instances take this to mean the contents are equivalent to 4 oz. (115 gm) of hops and apportion them accordingly.

Each recipe recommends using water to suit the type of beer being brewed. The recommended water treatments (if needed) are listed on page 26. Also most recipes call for the use of Irish moss, which, if no instructions are given, should be added during the last ten minutes of the boiling stage. Omitting the water treatment, Irish moss and gelatin finings will not stop you from brewing a good beer, but may prevent you from ending up with an excellent one true to type as I intended.

Skol Lager

RECIPE BASED ON SKOL LAGER BY CARLSBERG-TETLEY.

A very popular lager and one of the major selling brands. Lightly flavored with a refreshing bite.

Stage	25 quarts	Original gravity 1.034	25 liters
1	15 quarts	Water for lager brewing	15 liters
1	5 lb.	Crushed lager malt	2500 gm
1	3 oz.	Crashed wheat malt	100 gm
1	12 oz.	Flaked corn	400 gm
3	8 oz.	Brewing sugar	250 gm
3	1½ oz.	Hallertau hops	50 gm
3	1 oz.	Goldings hops	30 gm
3	1 tsp.	Irish moss	5 ml
5	2 oz.	Lager yeast	60 gm
5	½ oz.	Gelatin	15 gm
6	½ tsp./20 fl. oz.	White sugar	5 ml/liter

Brewing stages

1 Raise the temperature of the water to 104°F (40°C) and stir in the crushed malts and flaked corn. Stirring continuously, raise the mash temperature to 131°F (55°C). Let it stand for half an hour and then raise the temperature again to 151°F (66°C). Leave for 1½ hours, occasionally returning the temperature back to this value.

2 Pour the mashed grain into a large grain bag to retrieve the sweet wort. Using water slightly hotter than the mash, rinse the grains to collect 20 quarts (19 liters) of extract.

3 Boil the extract with the hops for 1½ hours. Dissolve the brewing sugar in a little hot water and add this during the boil. Also add the Irish moss as directed on the instructions.

4 Turn off the heat. Strain the clear wort into a fermenting bucket and add enough cold water to reach 25 quarts (25 liters).

5 When cool to room temperature, add the yeast. Ferment in a cool place (50°F [10°C]) until the specific gravity falls to 1.010. Rack into 5 quart (4.5 liter) jars or a 25 quart (24 liter) fermenter fitted with an airlock. Add gelatin before fitting airlocks.

6 Leave for 21 days before racking the beer from the sediment into primed beer bottles. Allow 30 days maturation before sampling. Serve chilled.

Brown Jack Best Brown Ale

RECIPE BASED ON BROWN JACK BEST
BROWN ALE BY ARKELL, SWINDON.

An excellent brown ale with a distinctive flavor of freshly roasted grain. The
deep garnet color topped with a fine white creamy head looks really impressive.

Stage	10 quarts	3.5% Alcohol	10 liters
1	2 lb.	Dark malt extract	1000 gm
1, 2	(2½+½) oz.	Crushed roast barley	(75 +15) gm
1	12 oz.	Brown sugar	400 gm
1	1 oz.	Fuggles hops	30 gm
1	10 quarts	Water for brown ale brewing	10 liters
2	2	Saccharin tablets	2
2	1 oz.	Home brew beer yeast	30 gm
3	½ tsp./20 fl. oz.	White sugar	5 ml/liter

Brewing stages

1 Boil the malt extract, first quota of roast barley and the hops in 10 quarts
(10 liters) of water for 45 minutes. Carefully strain the wort from the hops
and malt grains into a fermenting bucket. Rinse the spent grains and hops
with 2 pots of hot water. Dissolve the brown sugar in hot water and add
this to the bucket. Top up to 10 quarts (10 liters) with cold water.

2 When cool to room temperature, add the yeast, saccharin tablets and the
rest of the roast barley. Ferment 4–5 days until the activity abates. Rack
into secondary fermentation vessels and keep under airlock protection for
another 7 days.

3 Rack the beer off the sediment into primed beer bottles. Allow 10 days
maturation before sampling.

Carling Black Label

RECIPE BASED ON CARLING BLACK LABEL BY BASS.

British brewed version of a well-known Canadian brew.

Stage	25 quarts	Original gravity 1.039	25 liters
1	4½ lbs.	Crushed lager malt	2250 gm
1	15 quarts	Water for lager brewing	15 liters
3	2 lb.	White sugar	1000 gm
3	1 tsp.	Irish moss	5 ml
3	3 oz.	Hallertau hops	100 gm
5	2 oz.	Lager yeast	60 gm
5	½ oz.	Gelatin	15 gm
6	½ tsp./20 fl. oz.	Brown sugar	5 ml/liter

Brewing stages

1 Raise the temperature of the water to 113°F (45°C) and stir in the crushed malt. Stirring continuously, raise the mash temperature to 131°F (55°C). Let it stand for half an hour and then raise the temperature again to 151°F (66°C). Leave for one hour, occasionally returning the temperature back to this value.

2 Pour the mashed grain into a large grain bag to retrieve the sweet wort. Using water slightly hotter than the mash, rinse the grains to collect 20 quarts (19 liters) of extract.

3 Boil the extract with the hops for 1½ hours. Dissolve the white sugar in a little water and add this during the boil. Also add the Irish moss as directed on the instructions.

4 Turn off the heat. Strain the clear wort into a fermenting bucket and top up to 25 quarts (25 liters) with cold water.

5 When cool to room temperature, add the yeast. Ferment in a cool place until the specific gravity falls to 1.010. Rack into 5 quart (4.5 liter) jars or a secondary fermentation vessel fitted with an airlock. Add gelatin finings before fitting airlocks.

6 Leave for 21 days before racking the beer from the sediment into primed beer bottles. Allow 21 days maturation before sampling.

Bass or Toby Light Ale

RECIPE BASED ON BASS LIGHT ALE BY BASS.

Satisfying, appetizing, beery bouquet. Malty and hoppy in flavor bordering on pale ale characteristics. The Toby Jug was inspired by Toby Fillpot, the nickname for Henry Elwes the great glutton and star drunkard of the 18th century, who it is said consumed 24,000 gallons (90,850 liters) of ale in his lifetime.

Stage	25 quarts	Original gravity 1.035	25 liters
1	4¾ lb.	Crushed pale malt	2400 gm
1	12.5 quarts	Water for pale ale brewing	12 liters
3	1 tsp.	Irish moss	5 ml
3	12 oz.	Malt extract syrup	400 gm
3	8 oz.	Brown sugar	250 gm
3	2 oz.	Fuggles hops	60 gm
3	1½ oz.	Bramling Cross hops	45 gm
5	2 oz.	Brewer's yeast	60 gm
5	½ oz.	Gelatin	15 gm
6	½ tsp./20 fl. oz.	White sugar	5 ml/liter

Brewing stages

1 Raise the temperature of the water to 140°F (60°C) and stir in the crushed malt. Stirring continuously, raise the mash temperature to 151°F (66°C). Leave for 1½ hours, occasionally returning the temperature back to this value.

2 Pour the mashed grain into a large grain bag to retrieve the sweet wort. Using water slightly hotter than the mash, rinse the grains to collect 20 quarts (19 liters) of extract.

3 Boil the extract with the hops for 1½ hours. Dissolve the malt extract and the brown sugar in a little hot water and add this during the boil. Also add the Irish moss as directed on the instructions.

4 Turn off the heat, strain the clear wort into a fermenting bucket and top up to 25 quarts (25 liters) with cold water.

5 When cool to room temperature, add the yeast. Ferment 4–5 days until the specific gravity falls to 1.010. Rack into 5 quart (4.5 liter) jars or a 25 quart (24 liter) fermenter fitted with an airlock. Add gelatin finings before fitting airlocks.

6 Leave for 7 days before racking the beer from the sediment into primed beer bottles. Allow 10 days maturation before sampling.

Worthington White Shield

RECIPE BASED ON WORTHINGTON WHITE
SHIELD BY BASS, BIRMINGHAM.

One of the few naturally conditioned bottled beers brewed in the United
Kingdom and truly an esteemed ale of fine flavor and unblemished tradition.

Stage	20 quarts	Original gravity 1.052	20 liters
1	6½ lb.	Crushed pale malt	3250 gm
1	6 oz.	Crushed crystal malt	200 gm
1	15 quarts	Water for pale ale brewing	15 liters
3	1 tsp.	Irish moss	5 ml
3	1 lb.	Brewing sugar	500 gm
3	2 oz.	Fuggles hops	60 gm
3, 4, 5	(1+½ + ¼) oz.	Goldings hops	(30 +15 + 10) gm
5	½ oz.	Gelatin	15 gm
5		Yeast starter from bottle-conditioned beer	
6	½ tsp./20 fl. oz.	White sugar	5 ml /liter

Brewing stages

1 Raise the temperature of the water to 140°F (60°C) and stir in the crushed malts. Stirring continuously, raise the mash temperature up to 151°F (66°C). Leave for 1½ hours occasionally returning the temperature back to this value.

2 Pour the mashed grain into a large grain bag to retrieve the sweet wort. Using water slightly hotter than the mash, rinse the grains to collect 20 quarts (19 liters) of extract.

3 Boil the extract with the Fuggles hops and the first quota of Goldings hops for 1½ hours. Dissolve the brewing sugar in a little hot water and add this during the boil. Also add the Irish moss as directed on the instructions.

4 Turn off the heat, stir in the second batch of Goldings and allow the hops to soak for 15 minutes. Strain off the clear wort into a fermenting bucket and top up to 20 quarts (20 liters) with cold water.

5 When cool to room temperature, add the yeast. Ferment 4–5 days until the specific gravity falls to 1.012. Rack into 5 quart (4.5 liter) jars or a secondary fermentation vessel fitted with an airlock. Add gelatin and the rest of the dry hops before fitting airlocks.

6 Leave for 5 days before racking the beer from the sediment into primed beer bottles. Allow 21 days conditioning before sampling.

Special Brew Lager

**RECIPE BASED ON SPECIAL BREW LAGER
BY CARLSBERG, NORTHAMPTON.***

A very strong beautifully balanced beer; the lager equivalent of our barley wines. Backed by the best of Danish brewing experience, this lager is really a special brew.

Stage	15 quarts	Original gravity 1.080	15 liters
1	5¾ lb.	Crushed lager malt	2900 gm
1	1½ lb.	Flaked corn	750 gm
1	15 quarts	Water for lager brewing	15 liters
3	1 tsp.	Irish moss	5 ml
3	1½ lb.	Cane syrup	750 gm
3,4	(2½ + ½) oz.	Hallertau hops	(75 + 15) gm
5	1 oz.	Lager yeast	30 gm
5	½ oz.	Gelatin	15 gm
6	½ tsp./20 fl. oz.	White sugar	5 ml/liter

Brewing stages

1 Raise the temperature of the water to 113°F (45°C) and stir in the crushed malt and flaked corn. Stirring continuously, raise the mash temperature to 131°F (55°C). Let it stand for half an hour and then raise the temperature again to 151°F (66°C). Leave for 1½ hours, occasionally returning the temperature back to this value.

2 Pour the mashed grain into a large grain bag to retrieve the sweet wort. Using water slightly hotter than the mash, rinse the grains to collect 15 quarts (15 liters) of extract.

3 Boil the extract with the hops for 1½ hours. Dissolve the syrup in a little hot water and add this during the boil. Also add the Irish moss as directed on the instructions.

4 Turn off the heat, stir in the second batch of hops and allow them to soak for 15 minutes. Strain off the clear wort into a fermenting bucket and top up to 15 quarts (15 liters) with cold water.

5 When cool to room temperature, add the yeast. Ferment until the specific gravity falls to 1.020. Rack into 5 quart (4.5 liter) jars. Add gelatin and top up before fitting airlocks.

6 Leave for 30 days before racking the beer from the sediment into primed beer bottles. Allow 30 days conditioning before sampling. Chill before serving.

On top of the highly sophisticated brewing control pane at Carlsberg's Northampton Brewery is a glass case containing a Lager Beer Kit with a notice "In an emergency break glass and use!"

Imperial Russian Stout

**RECIPE BASED ON IMPERIAL RUSSIAN STOUT BY COURAGE,
CURRENTLY PRODUCED BY WELLS & YOUNG BREWING COMPANY.**

A beautifully smooth, naturally conditioned, dark barley wine originally brewed for the Tsarist Court where it found favor in the 18th century. The strongest beer regularly brewed in the United Kingdom.

Stage	10 quarts	Original gravity 1.103	10 liters
1	6 lb.	Crushed pale malt	3000 gm
1	½ lb.	Crushed crystal malt	250 gm
1	¼ lb.	Crushed chocolate malt	125 gm
1	¼ lb.	Crushed black malt	125 gm
1	15 quarts	Water for barley wine brewing	15 liters
3	1 lb.	Dark brown sugar	500 gm
3	3 oz.	Fuggles hops	100 gm
4	½ oz.	Wine yeast	15 gm
6	½ tsp./20 fl. oz.	White sugar	5 ml/liter

Brewing stages

1 Raise the temperature of the water to 140°F (60°C) and stir in the crushed malts. Stirring continuously, raise the mash temperature to 151°F (66°C). Leave for 1½ hours occasionally returning the temperature back to this value.

2 Pour the mashed grain into a large grain bag to retrieve the sweet wort. Using water slightly hotter than the mash, slowly and gently rinse the grains to collect 17.5 quarts (16 liters) of extract.

3 Boil the extract with the hops and the brown sugar dissolved in a little water until the volume has been reduced to slightly more than 10 quarts (10 liters). Strain off and divide equally among three 5 quart (4.5 liter) jars. Fit airlocks.

4 When cool, add wine yeast and ferment until the vigorous activity abates. Then, siphon into two 5 quart (4.5 liter) jars, filling each to the base of the neck. Refit airlocks and check regularly to ensure they don't dry out.

5 It will take months to complete the fermentation, after which the stout should be racked again, taking with it a minute quantity of the yeast sediment.

6 Store for six months before bottling in primed beer bottles (preferably small bottles around 7 fl. oz. [207ml]).

7 Mature for 18 months before sampling.

Konig Pilsner

RECIPE BASED ON KONIG PILSNER BY ELDRIDGE POPE, DORCHESTER.

Well-established English brewed lager that has been around long before the current surge in popularity of European styled beers.

Stage	25 quarts	Original gravity 1.035	25 liters
1	5 lb.	Crushed lager malt	2500 gm
1	1 lb.	Flaked rice	500 gm
1	15 quarts	Water for lager brewing	15 liters
3	8 oz.	Brewing sugar	250 gm
3	1½ oz.	Hallertau hops	45 gm
3	½ oz.	Goldings hops	15 gm
3	1 tsp.	Irish moss	5 ml
5	2 oz.	Lager yeast	60 gm
5	½ oz.	Gelatin	15 gm
6	½ tsp./20 fl. oz.	White sugar	5 ml/liter

Brewing stages

1 Raise the temperature of the water to 113°F (45°C) and stir in the crushed malt and flaked rice. Stirring continuously, raise the mash temperature to 131°F (55°C). Let it stand for half an hour and then raise the temperature again to 151°F (66°C). Leave for 1½ hours occasionally returning the temperature back to this value.

2 Pour the mashed grain into a large grain bag to retrieve the sweet wort. Using water slightly hotter than the mash, rinse the grains to collect 20 quarts (19 liters) of extract.

3 Boil the extract with the hops for 1½ hours. Dissolve the brewer's sugar in a little hot water and add this during the boil. Also add the Irish moss as directed on the instructions.

4 Turn off the heat. Strain the clear wort into a fermenting bucket and top up to 25 quarts (25 liters) with cold water.

5 When cool to room temperature, add the yeast. Ferment in a cool place until the specific gravity falls to 1.010. Rack into 5 quart (4.5 liter) jars or a 25 quart (24 liter) fermenter fitted with an airlock. Add gelatin before fitting airlocks.

6 Leave for 21 days before racking the beer from the sediment into primed beer bottles. Allow 30 days conditioning before sampling.

Thomas Hardy Ale

RECIPE BASED ON THOMAS HARDY ALE
BY ELDRIDGE POPE, DORCHESTER

The Dorset brewers celebrated the centenary of the birth of Wessex novelist Thomas Hardy in 1969 by creating this fine brew and bottling it in old Victorian bottles.

Thomas Hardy's immortal words still apply: "It was of the most beautiful color that the eye of an artist in beer could desire; full of body; yet brisk as a volcano; piquant, yet without a twang; luminous as an autumn sunset; free from streakiness of taste; but, finally rather heady."

Stage	10 quarts	Original gravity 1.120	10 liters
1	7 lb.	Crushed pale malt	3500 gm
1	1 lb.	Crushed lager malt	500 gm
1	15 quarts	Water for barley wine brewing	15 liters
3	1 lb.	Brewing sugar	500 gm
3	4 oz.	Goldings hops	125 gm
4	½ oz.	Wine yeast	15 gm
6	½ tsp./20 fl. oz.	White sugar	5 ml/liter

Brewing Stages

1 Raise the temperature of the water to 140°F (60°C) and stir in the crushed malts. Stirring continuously, raise the mash temperature to 151°F (66°C). Leave for 1½ hours occasionally returning the temperature back to this value.

2 Pour the mashed grain into a large grain bag to retrieve the sweet wort. Using water slightly hotter than the mash, slowly and gently rinse the grains to collect 17.5 quarts (16 liters) of extract.

3 Boil the extract with the hops and the brewing sugar dissolved in a little water until the volume has been reduced to slightly more than 10 quarts (10 liters). Strain and divide equally among three 5 quart (4.5 liter) jars. Fit airlocks.

4 When cool, add wine yeast and ferment until the vigorous activity abates. Then, siphon into two 5 quart (4.5 liter) jars, filling each to the base of the neck. Refit airlocks, and check regularly to ensure they don't dry out.

5 It will take months to complete the fermentation, after which the ale should be racked again, taking with it a minute quantity of the yeast sediment.

6 Store for six months before bottling in primed beer bottles and mature for 18 months before sampling.

Prize Old Ale

RECIPE BASED ON PRIZE OLE ALE BY GALES, HORNDEAN.

Based on an old Yorkshire recipe, an impressively mature barley wine of the highest quality. I am yet to come across another beer that gets such careful and lavish attention by the brewery. After brewing, the naturally conditioned ale is matured in oak casks for 12 months before bottling. Even then, it is recommended you keep it for another few years before sampling.

59

The following recipe is as near as I can get—and probably as near as I will get to this supreme ale.

Stage	10 quarts	Original gravity 1.100	10 liters
1	6½ lb.	Crushed pale malt	3250 gm
1	1 lb.	Crushed crystal malt	500 gm
1	1 oz.	Crushed black malt	30 gm
1	15 quarts	Water for barley wine brewing	15 liters
3	4 oz.	Molasses	125 gm
3	3¾ oz.	Goldings hops	120 gm
4	1 oz.	Wine yeast	30 gm
6	½ tsp./20 fl. oz.	White sugar	5 ml/liter

Brewing Stages

1   Raise the temperature of the water to 140°F (60°C) and stir in the crushed malts. Stirring continuously, raise the mash temperature to 151°F (66°C). Leave for 1½ hours occasionally returning the temperature back to 151°F (66°C).

2   Pour the mashed grain into a large grain bag to retrieve the sweet wort. Using water slightly hotter than the mash, slowly and gently rinse the grains to collect 17.5 quarts (16 liters) of extract.

3   Boil the extract with the hops and the molasses dissolved in a little water until the volume has been reduced to slightly more than 10 quarts (10 liters). Strain and divide equally among three 5 quart (4.5 liter) jars. Fit airlocks.

4   When cool, add wine yeast and ferment until the vigorous activity abates. Then siphon into two 5 quart (4.5 liter) jars, filling each to the base of the neck. Refit airlocks, and check regularly to ensure they don't dry out.

5   It will take months to complete the fermentation, after which the ale should be racked again, taking with it a minute quantity of the yeast sediment.

6   Store for six months before bottling in primed beer bottles and mature for 18 months before sampling.

Pale Ale

RECIPE BASED ON PALE ALE BY GREENE KING, BURY ST. EDMUNDS.

I rate Greene King as the best brewer of bottled ales in the United Kingdom, sporting ten excellent, but very different and distinct, ales.

The Pale Ale has a strong beautiful bouquet from the malt and hops and a luscious hoppy flavor.

Stage	25 quarts	3.4% Alcohol	25 liters
1	3 lb.	Light malt extract syrup	1500 gm
1	12 oz.	Crushed crystal malt	400 gm
1	1 lb.	Dark brown sugar	500 gm
1	1 ½ oz.	Northern Brewer hops	45 gm
1	2 oz.	Goldings hops	60 gm
1	1 tsp.	Irish moss	5 ml
1	5 quarts	Water for pale ale brewing	10 liters
2	2 oz.	Brewer's yeast	60 gm
2	½ oz.	Gelatin	15 gm
3	½ tsp./20 fl. oz.	White sugar	5 ml/liter

Brewing stages

1 Boil the malt extract, malt and hops for 45 minutes. Carefully strain the wort from the hops and malt grains into a fermenting bucket. Rinse the spent grains and hops with 2 pots of hot water. Dissolve the brown sugar in hot water and add this to the bucket. Top up to the final quantity with cold water.

2 When cool to room temperature, add the yeast. Ferment 4–5 days until the activity abates. Rack into secondary fermentation vessels and keep under airlock protection for another 7 days. Add gelatin and keep the beer under airlock protection for another 7 days.

3 Rack the beer off the sediment into primed beer bottles. Allow 10 days maturation before sampling.

Strong Pale Ale

RECIPE BASED ON STRONG PALE ALE BY
GREENE KING, BURY ST EDMUNDS.

Impressively smooth, sweetish ale that leaves no doubt about its strength!

Stage	20 quarts	Original gravity 1.060	20 liters
1	7 lb.	Crashed pale malt	3500 gm
1	8 oz.	Crushed crystal malt	250 gm
1	10 quarts	Water for pale ale brewing	10 liters
3	1 lb.	Raw brown sugar	500 gm
3	2 oz.	Molasses	60 gm
3	3 oz.	Goldings hops	100 gm
3	1 oz.	Northern Brewer hops	30 gm
3	1 tsp.	Irish moss	5 ml
5	2 oz.	Brewer's yeast	60 gm
5	½ oz.	Gelatin	15 gm
6	½ tsp./20 fl. oz.	White sugar	5 ml/liter

Brewing stages

1 Raise the temperature of the water to 140°F (60°C) and stir in the crushed malts. Stirring continuously, raise the mash temperature to 151°F (66°C). Leave for 1½ hours occasionally returning the temperature back to this value.

2 Pour the mashed grain into a large grain bag to retrieve the sweet wort. Using water slightly hotter than the mash, rinse the grains to collect 20 quarts (19 liters) of extract.

3 Boil the extract with the hops for 1½ hours. Dissolve the brown sugar and molasses in a little hot water and add this during the boil. Also add the Irish moss as directed on the instructions.

4 Turn off the heat and strain the clear wort into a fermenting bucket and top up to 20 quarts (20 liters) with cold water.

5 When cool to room temperature, add the yeast. Ferment 4–5 days until the specific gravity falls to 1.015. Rack into 5 quart (4.5 liter) jars or a secondary fermentation vessel fitted with an airlock. Add gelatin before fitting airlocks.

6 Leave for 7 days before racking the beer from the sediment into primed beer bottles. Allow 14 days conditioning before sampling.

Suffolk Strong Ale

RECIPE BASED ON SUFFOLK STRONG ALE
BY GREENE KING, BURY ST. EDMUNDS.

My favorite Pale Ale of Greene King's trio. Well matured flavor and bouquet of malt. Darker in color and less sweet than the Strong Ale version.

Stage	25 quarts	Original gravity 1.060	25 liters
1	6½ lb.	Crushed pale malt	3500 gm
1	1 lb.	Light malt extract syrup	500 gm
1	1 oz.	Crushed black malt	30 gm
1	15 quarts	Water for pale ale brewing	15 liters
3	1 lb.	Dark brown sugar	500 gm
3	2½ oz.	Goldings hops	75 gm
3	1 oz.	Northern Brewer hops	30 gm
3	2 oz.	Molasses	60 gm
3	1 tsp.	Irish moss	5 ml
4	½ oz.	Beer yeast	15 gm
6	½ tsp./20 fl. oz.	White sugar	5 ml/liter
6	15 quarts	Pale ale	15 liters

Brewing stages

1 Raise the temperature of the water to 140°F (60°C) and stir in the crushed malts and extract syrup. Stirring continuously, raise the mash temperature to 151°F (66°C). Leave for 1½ hours, occasionally returning the temperature back to this value.

2 Pour the mashed grain into a large grain bag to retrieve the sweet wort. Using water slightly hotter than the mash, slowly and gently rinse the grains to collect 15 quarts (15 liters) of extract.

3 Boil the extract with the hops and the brown sugar and molasses dissolved in a little water until the volume has been reduced to slightly more than 10 quarts (10 liters). Strain and divide equally among three 5 quart (4.5 liter) jars. Fit airlocks.

4 When cool, add a beer yeast and ferment until the vigorous activity abates. Then siphon into two 5 quart (4.5 liter) jars, filling each to the base of the neck. Refit airlocks, and check regularly to ensure they don't dry out.

5 It will take months to complete the fermentation, after which the ale should be racked again, taking with it a minute quantity of the yeast sediment. Store for 18 months.

6 Rack the ale into a 25 quart (24 liter) fermenter fitted with an airlock and add to it some freshly brewed Pale Ale (see page 62) taken after Stage 2 of that recipe. Stir thoroughly to mix the two brews and then bottle in primed beer bottles.

7 Mature for 28 days before sampling.

Harvest Brown Ale

63

RECIPE BASED ON HARVEST BROWN ALE BY
GREENE KING, BURY ST. EDMUNDS.

Typical Brown Ale—very dark red color, medium sweetness with distinctive hops to balance the maltiness of the brew.

Stage	15 quarts	3.6% Alcohol	25 liters
1	2 lb.	Diastatic malt extract	1000 gm
1	2½ oz.	Crushed black malt	75 gm
1	2 oz.	Crushed crystal malt	60 gm
1	1 lb.	Dark brown sugar	500 gm
1	1 oz.	Northern Brewer hops	30 gm
1	1 oz.	Fuggles hops	30 gm
1	10 quarts	Water for brown ale brewing	10 liters
2	½ oz.	Home brew beer yeast	15 gm
2	5	Saccharin tablets	5
3	½ tsp./20 fl. oz.	White sugar	5ml/liter

Brewing stages

1 Boil the malt extract, crushed malts, and hops in water for 45 minutes. Carefully strain the wort from the hops and malt grains into a fermenting bucket. Rinse the spent grains and hops with two pots of hot water. Dissolve the brown sugar in hot water and add this to the bucket. Top up to 15 quarts (15 liters) with cold water.

2 When cool to room temperature, add the yeast and saccharin tablets. Ferment 4–5 days until the activity abates. Rack into secondary fermentation vessels and keep under airlock protection for another 7 days.

3 Rack the beer off the sediment into primed beer bottles. Allow 10 days conditioning before sampling.

Harp Pilsner

RECIPE BASED ON HARP PILSNER BY HARP.

Once the best selling lager in the United Kingdom and a most widely distributed lager in Ireland, where sold on draft, the beer is conditioned with nitrogen to give a smooth but refreshing flavor and a nice creamy head. Canned Harp initially tastes of the can, but this off-flavor seems to dissipate quickly.

Stage	25 quarts	Original gravity 1.034	25 liters
1	5½ lb.	Crushed lager malt	2800 gm
1	1 lb.	Flaked corn	500 gm
1	15 quarts	Water for lager brewing	15 liters
3	2½ oz.	Hallertau hops	75 gm
3	1 tsp.	Irish moss	5 ml
3	½ tsp.	Brewer's caramel	3 ml
5	2 oz.	Lager yeast	60 gm
5	½ oz.	Gelatin	15 gm
6	½ tsp./20 fl. oz.	White sugar	5 ml/liter

Brewing stages

1. Raise the temperature of the water to 113°F (45°C) and stir in the crushed malt and flaked corn. Stirring continuously, raise the mash temperature to 131°F (55°C). Let it stand for half an hour and then raise the temperature again to 151°F (66°C). Leave for 1½ hours occasionally returning the temperature back to this value.

2. Pour the mashed grain into a large grain bag to retrieve the sweet wort. Using water slightly hotter than the mash, rinse the grains to collect 20 quarts (19 liters) of extract.

3. Boil the extract with the hops and caramel for 1½ hours. Also add the Irish moss as directed on the instructions.

4. Turn off the heat. Strain the clear wort into a fermenting bucket and top up to the final quantity with cold water.

5. When cool to room temperature, add the yeast. Ferment in a cool place until the specific gravity falls to 1.010. Rack into 5 quart (4.5 liter) jars or a 25 quart (24 liter) fermenter fitted with an airlock. Add gelatin before fitting airlocks.

6. Leave for 21 days before racking the beer from the sediment into primed beer bottles. Allow 30 days conditioning before sampling. Serve chilled.

Long Life

RECIPE BASED ON LONG LIFE BY IND, COOPE & CO. (CARLSBERG-TETLEY), BURTON-ON-TRENT.

In sampling this brew, I was not sure whether to classify it as a lager or a light ale. It is a very distinctive and palatable beer and that is all that really matters.

Stage	25 quarts	Original gravity 1.041	25 liters
1	6 lb.	Crushed pale malt	3000 gm
1	1½ lb.	Flaked corn	750 gm
1	4 oz.	Crushed wheat malt	125 gm
1	15 quarts	Water for lager brewing	15 liters
3	1 tsp.	Irish moss	5 ml
3	1 tsp.	Brewer's caramel	5 ml
3	2 oz.	Hallertau hops	60 gm
5	1 oz. (equiv.)	Hop extract	30 gm (equiv.)
5	2 oz.	Lager yeast	60 gm
5	½ oz.	Gelatin	15 gm
6	½ tsp./20 fl. oz.	White sugar	5 ml/liter

Brewing stages

1 Raise the temperature of the water to 140°F (60°C) and stir in the crushed malts and flaked corn. Stirring continuously, raise the mash temperature to 151°F (66°C). Leave for 1½ hours occasionally returning the temperature back to this value.

2 Pour the mashed grain into a large grain bag to retrieve the sweet wort. Using water slightly hotter than the mash, rinse the grains to collect 20 quarts (19 liters) of extract.

3 Boil the extract with the Hallertau hops and caramel for 1½ hours. Also add the Irish moss as directed on the instructions.

4 Turn off the heat. Strain the clear wort into a fermenting bucket and top up to the final quantity with cold water.

5 When cool to room temperature, add the yeast and hop extract. Ferment in a cool place until the specific gravity falls to 1.012. Rack into 5 quart (4.5 liter) jars or a secondary fermentation vessel fitted with an airlock. Add gelatin before fitting airlocks.

6 Leave for 14 days before racking the beer from the sediment into primed beer bottles. Allow 21 days maturation before sampling.

Light Ale

RECIPE BASED ON LIGHT ALE BY IND, COOPE & CO. (CARLSBERG-TETLEY), BURTON-ON-TRENT.

Looks more like a bitter beer and taste is bordering on it as well.

Stage	25 quarts	3.5% Alcohol	25 liters
1	2 lb.	Diastatic malt extract	1000 gm
1	8 oz.	Crushed crystal malt	250 gm
1	2 lb.	Raw brown sugar	1000 gm
1	1½ oz.	Fuggles hops	45 gm
1	10 quarts	Water for light ale brewing	10 liters
2	1 oz.	Home brew beer yeast	30 gm
2	½ oz.	Gelatin	15 gm
3	½ tsp./20 fl. oz.	White sugar	5 ml/liter

Brewing stages

1 Boil the malt extract, crystal malt and hops in water for 45 minutes. Carefully strain the wort from the hops and malt grains into a fermenting bucket. Rinse the spent grains and hops with two pots of hot water. Dissolve the brown sugar in hot water and add this to the bucket. Top up to the final quantity with cold water.

2 When cool to room temperature, pitch in the yeast. Ferment 4–5 days until the activity abates. Rack into secondary fermentation vessels and keep under airlock protection for another seven days. Add gelatin and keep the beer under airlock protection for another seven days.

3 Rack the beer off the sediment into primed beer bottles. Allow 10 days maturation before sampling.

Export I. P. A.

RECIPE BASED ON EXPORT INDIAN PALE ALE, NOW KNOWN AS MCEWAN'S INDIA PALE ALE BY MCEWAN'S (SCOTTISH & NEWCASTLE).

Popular beer. Thick, malty flavor kept smooth through relatively low carbonation. Nice frothy head that lasts.

67

Stage	25 quarts	Original gravity 1.045	25 liters
1	6 lb.	Crashed pale malt	3000 gm
1	1 lb.	Flaked barley	500 gm
1	½ oz.	Crushed black malt	15 gm
1	15 quarts	Water for pale ale brewing	15 liters
3	1 tsp.	Irish moss	5 ml
3	1 lb.	Dark brown sugar	500 gm
3	2 oz.	Hallertau hops	60 gm
5	1 oz. (equiv.)	Hop extract	30 gm (equiv.)
5	2 oz.	Brewer's yeast	60 gm
5	½ oz.	Gelatin	15 gm
6	½ tsp./20 fl. oz.	White sugar	5 ml/liter

Brewing stages

1 Raise the temperature of the water to 140°F (60°C) and stir in the crushed malts and barley flakes. Stirring continuously, raise the mash temperature to 151°F (66°C). Leave for 1½ hours occasionally returning the temperature back to this value.

2 Pour the mashed grain into a large grain bag to retrieve the sweet wort. Using water slightly hotter than the mash, rinse the grains to collect 20 quarts (19 liters) of extract.

3 Boil the extract with the Hallertau hops for 1½ hours. Dissolve the brown sugar in a little hot water and add this during the boil. Also add the Irish moss as directed on the instructions.

4 Turn off the heat and strain the clear wort into a fermenting bucket and top up to the final quantity with cold water.

5 When cool to room temperature, add the yeast and hop extract. Ferment 4–5 days until the specific gravity falls to 1.012. Rack into 5 quart (4.5 liter) jars or a 25 quart (24 liter) fermenter fitted with an airlock. Add gelatin before fitting airlocks.

6 Leave for 7 days before racking the beer from the sediment into primed beer bottles. Allow 10 days maturation before sampling.

Newcastle Amber Ale

**RECIPE BASED ON NEWCASTLE AMBER ALE BY SCOTTISH &
NEWCASTLE, NOW OWNED BY HEINEKEN AND CARLSBERG.**

A light, refreshing ale, in many ways styled on the better-known Brown
Ale version.

68

Stage	25 quarts	3.2% Alcohol	25 liters
1	2½ lb.	Diastatic malt extract	1250 gm
1	6 oz.	Crushed crystal malt	200 gm
1	1 lb.	Brown sugar	500 gm
1	1 lb.	Coffee sugar crystals	500 gm
1	1 oz.	Fuggles hops	30 gm
1	10 quarts	Water for light ale brewing	10 liters
2	1½ oz. (equiv.)	Hop extract	45 gm (equiv.)
2	1 oz.	Home brew beer yeast	30 gm
2	½ oz.	Gelatin	15 gm
3	½ tsp./20 fl. oz.	White sugar	5 ml/liter

Brewing stages

1 Boil the malt extract, malt and hops in water for 45 minutes. Carefully
strain the wort from the hops and malt grains into a fermenting bucket.
Rinse the spent grains and hops with two pots of hot water. Dissolve the
coffee sugar crystals and brown sugar in hot water and add this to the
bucket. Top up to the final quantity with cold water.

2 When cool to room temperature, add the yeast and hop extract. Ferment
4–5 days until the activity abates. Rack into secondary fermentation
vessels. Add gelatin and keep the beer under airlock protection for another
7 days.

3 Rack the beer off the sediment into primed beer bottles Allow 10 days
maturation before sampling.

Newcastle Brown Ale

RECIPE BASED ON NEWCASTLE BROWN ALE BY SCOTTISH & NEWCASTLE, NOW OWNED BY HEINEKEN AND CARLSBERG.

"Geordie Champagne" as it is affectionately called, is probably the best-known Northern beer. A unique brown ale, light in color, heavy in strength and flavor and easily recognized in its clear bottles. Celebrated its 50th Jubilee in 1977.

Stage	25 quarts	Original gravity 1.048	25 liters
1	7 lb.	Crashed pale malt	3500 gm
1	8 oz.	Crushed crystal malt	250 gm
1	3 oz.	Crushed chocolate malt	100 gm
1	15 quarts	Water for strong ale brewing	15 liters
3	1 tsp.	Irish moss	5 ml
3	1 lb.	Dark brown sugar	500 gm
3	2 oz.	Fuggles hops	60 gm
5	5	Saccharin tablets	5
5	1½ oz. (equiv.)	Hop extract (Northern Brewer)	50 gm (equiv.)
5	2 oz.	Brewer's yeast	60 gm
5	½ oz.	Gelatin	15 gm
6	½ tsp./20 fl. oz.	White sugar	5 ml/liter

Brewing stages

1 Raise the temperature of the water to 140°F (60°C) and stir in the crushed malts. Stirring continuously, raise the mash temperature to 151°F (66°C). Leave for 1½ hours occasionally returning the temperature back to 151°F (66°C).

2 Pour the mashed grain into a large grain bag to retrieve the sweet wort. Using water slightly hotter than the mash, rinse the grains to collect 20 quarts (19 liters) of extract.

3 Boil the extract with the Fuggles hops for 1½ hours. Dissolve the brown sugar in a little hot water and add this during the boil. Add the Irish moss as directed on the instructions.

4 Turn off the heat and strain the clear wort into a fermenting bucket. Top up to the final quantity with cold water.

5 When cool to room temperature, add the yeast, hop extract and saccharin tablets. Ferment 4–5 days until the specific gravity falls to 1.012. Rack into 5 quart (4.5 liter) jars or a 25 quart (24 liter) fermenter fitted with an airlock. Add gelatin before fitting airlocks.

6 Leave for 7 days before racking the beer from the sediment into primed beer bottles. Allow 14 days conditioning before sampling.

Extra Stout

RECIPE BASED ON EXTRA STOUT BY PALMERS, BRIDPORT.

Most enjoyable stout, well balanced and tasty.

Stage	25 quarts	Original gravity 1.036	25 liters
1	5 lb.	Crushed pale malt	2500 gm
1	8 oz.	Crushed crystal malt	250 gm
1	6 oz.	Crushed black malt	200 gm
1	12.5 quarts	Water for sweet stout brewing	12 liters
3	2 oz.	Fuggles hops	60 gm
3	1 lb.	Dark brown sugar	500 gm
3	1 tsp.	Irish Moss	5 ml
5	2 oz.	Brewer's yeast	60 gm
6	½ tsp./20 fl. oz.	White sugar	5 ml/liter

Brewing stages

1 Raise the temperature of the water to 140°F (60°C) and stir in the crushed malts. Stirring continuously raise the mash temperature to 151°F (66°C). Leave for 1½ hours occasionally returning the temperature back to this value.

2 Pour the mashed grain into a large grain bag to retrieve the sweet wort. Using water slightly hotter than the mash, rinse the grains to collect 20 quarts (19 liters) of extract.

3 Boil the extract with the hops for 1½ hours. Dissolve the brown sugar in a little hot water and add this during the boil. Add some Irish moss as directed on the instructions.

4 Turn off the heat. Strain the clear wort into a fermenting bucket and top up to the final quantity with cold water.

5 When cool to room temperature, add the yeast. Ferment 4–5 days until the specific gravity falls to 1.010. Rack into 5 quart (4.5 liter) jars or a 25 quart (24 liter) fermenter fitted with an airlock.

6 Leave for 7 days before racking the beer from the sediment into primed beer bottles. Allow 45 days conditioning before sampling.

Sainsbury Light Ale

RECIPE BASED ON LIGHT ALE BY J. SAINSBURY, PLC. (SUPERMARKET).

Excellent beery, hoppy aroma. Low carbonation level keeps the flavor smooth and plentiful without incurring too much bitterness from the generous quota of hops.

Stage	25 quarts	Original gravity 1.030	25 liters
1	5 lb.	Crushed pale malt	2500 gm
1	5 oz.	Crushed crystal malt	150 gm
1	12.5 quarts	Water for light ale brewing	12 liters
3	1 oz.	Fuggles hops	30 gm
3, 4, 5	(2 + ¼ + ¼) oz.	Goldings hops	(60 +10 + 10) gm
3	1 tsp.	Irish moss	5 ml
3	6 oz.	Dark brown sugar	200 gm
5	2 oz.	Brewer's yeast	60 gm
5	½ oz.	Gelatin	15 gm
6	½ tsp./20 fl. oz.	White sugar	5 ml/liter

Brewing stages

1 Raise the temperature of the water to 140°F (60°C) and stir in the crushed malts. Stirring continuously, raise the mash temperature to 151°F (66°C). Leave for 1½ hours occasionally returning the temperature back to this value.

2 Pour the mashed grain into a large grain bag to retrieve the sweet wort. Using water slightly hotter than the mash, rinse the grains to collect 20 quarts (19 liters) of extract.

3 Boil the extract with the Fuggles hops and the first quota of Goldings hops for 1½ hours. Dissolve the brown sugar in a little hot water and add this during the boil. Add the Irish moss as directed on the instructions.

4 Turn off the heat, stir in the second batch of Goldings hops and allow them to soak for 15 minutes. Strain off the clear wort into a fermenting bucket and top up to the final quantity with cold water.

5 When cool to room temperature, add the yeast. Ferment 4–5 days until the specific gravity falls to 1.010. Rack into 5 quart (4.5 liter) jars or a secondary fermentation vessel fitted with an airlock. Add gelatin and the rest of the dry hops before fitting airlocks.

6 Leave for 7 days before racking the beer from the sediment into primed beer bottles. Allow 10 days maturation before sampling.

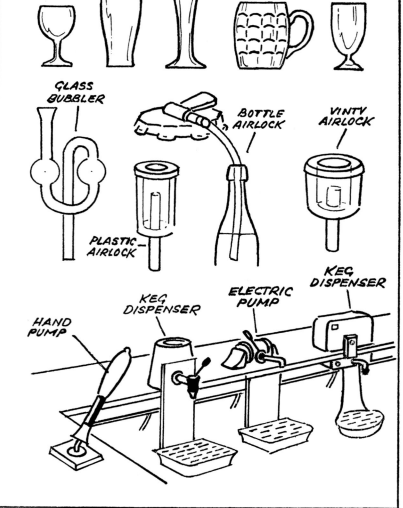

There are many different ways to ferment and serve beer. Here are just a few examples of the large variety of beer glasses, airlocks, and beer dispensers.

Lager

RECIPE BASED ON LAGER BY TENNENT (BASS), GLASGOW.

A good example of British lager brewing. Well hopped to give a satisfying flavor. Mind you it should be good, as Tennent have been experts in Lager brewing since 1888.

Stage	25 quarts	Original gravity 1.037	25 liters
1	5¼ lb.	Crushed lager malt	2700 gm
1	8 oz.	Flaked corn	250 gm
1	15 quarts	Water for lager brewing	15 liters
3	1 tsp.	Irish moss	5 ml
3	1 lb.	Blended honey	500 gm
3	2 oz.	Hallertau hops	60 gm
3	½ oz.	Goldings hops	15 gm
5	2 oz.	Lager yeast	60 gm
5	½ oz.	Gelatin	15 gm
6	½ tsp./20 fl. oz.	White sugar	5 ml/liter

Brewing stages

1 Raise the temperature of the water to 113°F (45°C) and stir in the crushed malt and corn flakes. Stirring continuously, raise the mash temperature to 131°F (55°C). Let it stand for half an hour and then raise the temperature again to 151°F (66°C). Leave for 1½ hours occasionally returning the temperature back to this value.

2 Pour the mashed grain into a large grain bag to retrieve the sweet wort. Using water slightly hotter than the mash, rinse the grains to collect 20 quarts (19 liters) of extract.

3 Boil the extract with the hops for 1½ hours. Dissolve the honey in a little hot water and add this during the boil. Also add the Irish moss as directed on the instructions.

4 Turn off the heat. Strain the clear wort into a fermenting bucket and top up to the final quantity with cold water.

5 When cool to room temperature, add the yeast. Ferment in a cool place until the specific gravity falls to 1.010. Rack into 5 quart (4.5 liter) jars or a 25 quart (24 liter) fermenter fitted with an airlock. Add gelatin before fitting airlocks.

6 Leave for 21 days before racking the beer from the sediment into primed beer bottles. Allow 30 days conditioning before sampling.

Pilsner Lager

RECIPE BASED ON PILSNER LAGER BY TUBORG (BASS).

A good-looking lager with a clean palate.

Stage	25 quarts	Original gravity 1.031	25 liters
1	4½ lb.	Crushed lager malt	2250 gm
1	14 oz.	Flaked corn	450 gm
1	9 oz.	Crushed wheat malt	275 gm
1	12.5 quarts	Water for lager brewing	12 liters
3	2 oz.	Hallertau hops	60 gm
3	1 tsp.	Irish moss	5 ml
5	2 oz.	Lager yeast	60 gm
5	½ oz.	Gelatin	15 gm
6	½ tsp./20 fl. oz.	White sugar	5 ml/liter

Brewing stages

1 Raise the temperature of the water to 113°F (45°C) and stir in the crushed malts and flaked corn. Stirring continuously, raise the mash temperature to 131°F (55°C). Let it stand for half an hour and then raise the temperature again to 151°F (66°C). Leave for 1 hour occasionally returning the temperature back to this value.

2 Pour the mashed grain into a large grain bag to retrieve the sweet wort. Using water slightly hotter than the mash, rinse the grains to collect 20 quarts (19 liters) of extract.

3 Boil the extract with the hops for 1½ hours. Also add the Irish moss as directed on the instructions.

4 Turn off the heat. Strain the clear wort into a fermenting bucket and top up to the final quantity with cold water.

5 When cool to room temperature, add the yeast. Ferment in a cool place until the specific gravity falls to 1.010. Rack into 5 quart (4.5 liter) jars or a secondary fermentation vessel fitted with an airlock. Add gelatin before fitting airlocks.

6 Leave for 21 days before racking the beer from the sediment into primed beer bottles. Allow 21 days maturation before sampling.

Watney's Cream Label

RECIPE BASED ON WATNEY'S CREAM LABEL BY WATNEY MANN.

Rich, luscious, sweet stout.

Stage	25 quarts	3.5% Alcohol	25 liters
1	3 lb.	Malt extract syrup	1500 gm
1	½ lb.	Crushed crystal malt	250 gm
1	½ lb.	Crushed black malt	250 gm
1	1 lb.	Brown sugar	500 gm
1	3 tsp.	Caramel	15 ml
1	1½ oz.	Fuggles hops	45 gm
1	15 quarts	Water for sweet stout brewing	15 liters
2	1 oz.	Home brew beer yeast	30 gm
2	10	Saccharin tablets	10
3	½ tsp./20 fl. oz.	White sugar	5 ml/liter

Brewing stages

1 Boil the malt extract, malts and hops in water for 45 minutes. Carefully strain the wort from the hops and malt grains into a fermenting bucket. Rinse the spent grains and hops with two pots of hot water. Dissolve the brown sugar and caramel in hot water and add this to the bucket. Top up to the final quantity with cold water.

2 When cool to room temperature, add the yeast and saccharin tablets. Ferment 4–5 days until the activity abates. Rack into secondary fermentation vessels and keep under airlock protection for another 7 days.

3 Rack the beer off the sediment into primed beer bottles. Allow 7 days maturation before sampling.

Mann's Brown Ale

RECIPE BASED ON MANN'S BROWN ALE BY WATNEY MANN.

A really smooth brown ale with a delicious malt flavor.

Stage	15 quarts	3.2% Alcohol	15 liters
1	2 lb.	Malt extract syrup	1000 gm
1	2 oz.	Crushed black malt	60 gm
1	1 lb.	Brewing sugar	500 gm
1	10 quarts	Water for brown ale brewing	10 liters
1	2 tsp.	Caramel	10 ml
1	½ oz.	Northern Brewer hops	15 gm
2	1 oz.	Home brew beer yeast	30 gm
2	1 oz. (equiv.)	Hop extract	30 gm (equiv.)
2	5	Saccharin tablets	5
3	½ tsp./20 fl. oz.	White sugar	5 ml/liter

Brewing stages

1 Boil malt extract, crushed malt and Northern Brewer hops in water for 45 minutes. Carefully strain the wort from the hops and malt grains into a fermenting bucket. Rinse the spent grains and hops with two pots of hot water. Dissolve the brewing sugar and caramel in hot water and add to the bucket. Top up to the final quantity with cold water.

2 When cool to room temperature, add the yeast, hop extract and saccharin tablets. Ferment 4–5 days until the activity abates. Rack into secondary fermentation vessels and keep under airlock protection for another 7 days.

3 Rack the beer off the sediment into primed beer bottles. Allow 10 days maturation before sampling.

Mackeson

RECIPE BASED ON MACKESON BY WHITBREAD.

"It looks good, tastes good, and by golly it does you good!" Dark, smooth, bitter, with a tremendous amount of flavor packed into one drink made it a firm favorite of thousands.

Stage	15 quarts	3.3% Alcohol	15 liters
1	2 lb.	Dark malt extract	1000 gm
1	4 oz.	Crushed chocolate malt	125 gm
1	1 lb.	Dark brown sugar	500 gm
1	4 tsp.	Brewer's caramel	20 ml
1	1 oz.	Fuggles hops	30 gm
1	1 oz.	Northern Brewer hops	30 gm
1	10 quarts	Water for stout brewing	10 liters
2	1 oz.	Home brew beer yeast	30 gm
2	5	Saccharin tablets	5
3	½ tsp./20 fl. oz.	White sugar	5 ml/liter

Brewing stages

1 Boil the malt extract, malt grains and hops in 10 quarts (10 liters) of water for 45 minutes. Carefully strain the wort from the hops and malt grains into a fermenting bucket. Rinse the spent grains and hops with two pots of hot water. Dissolve the caramel and sugar in hot water and add to the bucket. Top up to the final quantity with cold water.

2 When cool to room temperature, add the yeast and saccharin tablets. Ferment 4–5 days until the activity abates. Rack into secondary fermentation vessels and keep under airlock protection for another 7 days.

3 Rack the beer off the sediment into primed beer bottles. Allow 10 days maturation before sampling.

Heineken Pilsner Lager

RECIPE BASED ON HEINEKEN PILSNER LAGER BY WHITBREAD.

Good-looking lager with a fine creamy head with a balanced hop bite.

Stage	25 quarts	Original gravity 1.034	25 liters
1	5½ lb.	Crushed lager malt	2800 gm
1	14 oz.	Flaked rice	450 gm
1	3 oz.	Crushed crystal malt	100 gm
1	15 quarts	Water for lager brewing	15 liters
3	3 oz.	Hallertau hops	100 gm
3	1 tsp.	Irish moss	5 ml
5	2 oz.	Lager yeast	60 gm
5	½ oz.	Gelatin	15 gm
6	½ tsp./20 fl. oz.	White sugar	5 ml/liter

Brewing stages

1 Raise the temperature of the water to 113°F (45°C) and stir in the crushed malts and flaked rice. Stirring continuously, raise the mash temperature to 131°F (55°C). Let it stand for half an hour and then raise the temperature again to 151°F (66°C). Leave for 1½ hours occasionally returning the temperature back to this value.

2 Pour the mashed grain into a large grain bag to retrieve the sweet wort. Using water slightly hotter than the mash, rinse the grains to collect 20 quarts (19 liters) of extract.

3 Boil the extract with the hops for 1½ hours. Also add the Irish moss as directed on the instructions.

4 Turn off the heat. Strain the clear wort into a fermenting bucket and top up to the final quantity with cold water.

5 When cool to room temperature, add the yeast. Ferment in a cool place until the specific gravity falls to 1.010. Rack into 5 quart (4.5 liter) jars or a 25 quart (24 liter) fermenter fitted with an airlock. Add gelatin before fitting airlocks.

6 Leave for 21 days before racking the beer from the sediment into primed beer bottles. Allow 30 days conditioning before sampling.

Whitbread Light Ale

RECIPE BASED ON LIGHT ALE BY WHITBREAD.

Well-balanced characteristics for a light ale. Clean, refreshing with a nice flavor from the Northern Brewer hops.

Stage	25 quarts	Original gravity 1.034	25 liters
1	5 lb.	Crushed pale malt	2500 gm
1	5 oz.	Crushed crystal malt	150 gm
1	8 oz.	Flaked barley	250 gm
1	12.5 quarts	Water for light ale brewing	12 liters
3	2 oz.	Goldings hops	60 gm
3, 4	(¾ + ¾) oz.	Northern Brewer hops	(25 + 25) gm
3	8 oz.	Brewing sugar	250 gm
3	1 tsp.	Irish moss	5 ml
5	2 oz.	Brewer's yeast	60 gm
5	½ oz.	Gelatin	15 gm
6	½ tsp./20 fl. oz.	White sugar	5 ml/liter

Brewing stages

1 Raise the temperature of the water to 140°F (60°C) and stir in the crushed malts and barley. Stirring continuously, raise the mash temperature to 151°F (66°C). Leave for 1½ hours occasionally returning the temperature back to this value.

2 Pour the mashed grain into a large grain bag to retrieve the sweet wort. Using water slightly hotter than the mash, rinse the grains to collect 20 quarts (19 liters) of extract.

3 Boil the extract with the Goldings hops and the first quota of Northern Brewer hops for 1½ hours. Dissolve the brewing sugar in a little hot water and add this during the boil. Also add the Irish moss as directed on the instructions.

4 Turn off the heat, stir in the second batch of Northern Brewer hops and allow them to soak for 15 minutes. Strain the clear wort into a fermenting bucket and top up to the final quantity with cold water.

5 When cool to room temperature, add the yeast. Ferment 4–5 days until the specific gravity falls to 1.010. Rack into 5 quart (4.5 liter) jars or a 25 quart (24 liter) fermenter fitted with an airlock. Add gelatin before fitting airlocks.

6 Leave for 7 days before racking the beer from the sediment into primed beer bottles. Allow 10 days maturation before sampling.

'Wee Willie' Light Pale Ale

RECIPE BASED ON 'WEE WILLIE' PALE ALE BY YOUNGERS, EDINBURGH.

Nice nutty malt flavor carefully blended with strong hops to achieve palate balance.

Stage	25 quarts	Original gravity 1.036	25 liters
1	5 lb.	Crushed pale malt	2500 gm
1	6 oz.	Flaked barley	200 gm
1	15 quarts	Water for pale ale brewing	15 liters
3	2 tsp.	Brewer's caramel	10 ml
3	2 oz.	Fuggles hops	60 gm
3	1 oz.	Northern Brewer hops	30 gm
3	1 tsp.	Irish moss	5 ml
3	1 lb.	Brewing sugar	500 gm
5	2 oz.	Brewer's yeast	60 gm
5	½ oz.	Gelatin	15 gm
6	½ tsp./20 fl. oz.	White sugar	5 ml/liter

Brewing stages

1 Raise the temperature of the water to 140°F (60°C) and stir in the crushed malt and barley. Stirring continuously, raise the mash temperature to 151°F (66°C). Leave for 1½ hours occasionally returning the temperature back to this value.

2 Pour the mashed grain into a large grain bag to retrieve the sweet wort. Using water slightly hotter than the mash, rinse the grains to collect 20 quarts (19 liters) of extract.

3 Boil the extract with the hops for 1½ hours. Dissolve the brewing sugar and caramel in a little hot water and add this during the boil. Also add the Irish moss as directed on the instructions.

4 Turn off the heat. Strain the clear wort into a fermenting bucket and top up to the final quantity with cold water.

5 When cool to room temperature, add the yeast. Ferment 4–5 days until the specific gravity falls to 1.010. Rack into 5 quart (4.5 liter) jars or a secondary fermentation vessel, fitted with an airlock. Add gelatin before fitting airlocks.

6 Leave for 7 days before racking the beer from the sediment into primed beer bottles. Allow 10 days maturation before sampling.

Draft Beers and Real Ale

Southwold Bitter

RECIPE BASED ON SOUTHWOLD BITTER BY ADNAMS, SOUTHWOLD.

Good malty bitter; a favorite with real ale drinkers.

Stage	25 quarts	Original gravity 1.037	25 liters
1	6 lb.	Crushed pale malt	3000 gm
1	4 oz.	Crushed crystal malt	125 gm
1	2 oz.	Crushed roast barley	60 gm
1	15 quarts	Water for bitter brewing	15 liters
3	1 tsp.	Irish moss	5 ml
3	1 lb.	Brewing sugar	500 gm
3	2 oz.	Fuggles hops	60 gm
3, 4, 5	(1 + ½ + ¼) oz.	Goldings hops	(30 + 15 + 10) gm
5	2 oz.	Brewer's yeast	60 gm
5	½ oz.	Gelatin	15 gm
6	2 oz.	Brown sugar	60 gm

Brewing stages

1 Raise the temperature of the water to 140°F (60°C) and stir in the crushed malts and barley. Stirring continuously, raise the mash temperature to 151°F (66°C). Leave for 1½ hours occasionally returning the temperature back to this value.

2 Pour the mashed grain into a large grain bag to retrieve the sweet wort. Using water slightly hotter than the mash, rinse the grains to collect 20 quarts (19 liters) of extract.

3 Boil the extract with the Fuggles hops and the first quota of Goldings hops for 1½ hours. Dissolve the brewing sugar in a little hot water and add this during the boil. Also add the Irish moss as directed on the instructions.

4 Turn off the heat, stir in the second batch of Goldings hops and allow them to soak for 15 minutes. Strain the clear wort into a fermenting bucket and top up to the final quantity with cold water.

5 When cool to room temperature, add the yeast. Ferment 4–5 days until the specific gravity falls to 1.010. Rack into 5 quart (4.5 liter) jars or a 25 quart (24 liter) fermenter fitted with an airlock. Add gelatin and the rest of the dry hops before fitting airlocks.

6 Leave for 7 days before racking the beer from the sediment into a primed pressure barrel. Allow 7 days conditioning before sampling.

82

Cellar language.

- **Stillage:** chocks and supports for beer casks.

- **Soft peg:** porous peg that vents conditioning CO_2 from cask.

- **Ullage:** space in the barrel above the beer.

- **Bung:** Large cork fitting aperture in stave of cask.

- **Hard peg:** A long conical hardwood peg for insertionin

  in vent hole of shive to exclude air.

- **Shive:** Flat wooden plug fitting used to house pegs.

B. B. B. Bitter (3B)

RECIPE BASED ON 3B BY ARKELL, SWINDON.

A clean, crisp, hoppy brew. After a couple of glasses, I acquired quite a taste for this Swindon beer. My 25 quart (25 liter) batch went down just as well!

Stage	25 quarts	Original gravity 1.039	25 liters
1	5 lb. 10 oz.	Crushed pale malt	2850 gm
1	¾ oz.	Crushed roast barley	25 gm
1	12 oz.	Flaked corn	400 gm
1	15 quarts	Water for bitter brewing	15 liters
3	1 tsp.	Irish moss	5 ml
3	10 oz.	Brewing sugar	300 gm
3	½ oz.	Bramling Cross hops	15 gm
3	2 oz.	Fuggles hops	60 gm
4, 5	(½ + ¼) oz.	Goldings hops	(15 + 10) gm
5	2 oz.	Brewer's yeast	60 gm
5	½ oz.	Gelatin	15 gm
6	2 oz.	White sugar	60 gm

Brewing stages

1 Raise the temperature of the water to 140°F (60°C) and stir in the crushed malt, flaked corn and barley. Stirring continuously, raise the mash temperature to 151°F (66°C). Leave for 1½ hours occasionally returning the temperature back to this value.

2 Pour the mashed grain into a large grain bag to retrieve the sweet wort. Using water slightly hotter than the mash, rinse the grains to collect 20 quarts (19 liters) of extract.

3 Boil the extract with the Fuggles and Bramling Cross hops for 1½ hours. Dissolve the brewing sugar in a little hot water and add this during the boil. Also add the Irish moss as directed on the instructions.

4 Turn off the heat, stir in the first batch of Goldings hops and allow them to soak for 15 minutes. Strain off the clear wort into a fermenting bucket and top up to the final quantity with cold water.

5 When cool to room temperature, add the yeast. Ferment 4–5 days until the specific gravity falls to 1.010. Rack into 5 quart (4.5 liter) jars or a secondary fermentation vessel, fitted with an airlock. Add gelatin and the rest of the dry hops before fitting airlocks.

6 Leave for 5 days before racking the beer from the sediment into a primed pressure barrel. Allow 5 days conditioning before sampling.

Kingsdown Ale

RECIPE BASED ON KINGSDOWN ALE BY ARKELL, SWINDON.

This light, golden-colored, strong ale has a warm flavor. It is available in both bottled and draft versions.

Stage	25 quarts	Original gravity 1.060	25 liters
1	5 lb.	Crushed pale malt	2500 gm
1	2 oz.	Crushed black malt	60 gm
1	12.5 quarts	Water for strong ale brewing	12 liters
3	1 tsp.	Irish moss	5 ml
3	4 lb.	Malt extract syrup	2000 gm
3, 6	(14 + 2) oz.	Raw brown sugar	(450 + 50) gm
3	2 oz.	Fuggles hops	60 gm
3	2 oz.	Goldings hops	60 gm
5	5	Saccharin tablets	5
5	2 oz.	Brewer's yeast	60 gm
5	½ oz.	Gelatin	15 gm

Brewing stages

1 Raise the temperature of the water to 140°F (60°C) and stir in the crushed malts. Stirring continuously raise the mash temperature to 151°F (66°C). Leave for 1½ hours occasionally returning the temperature back to this value.

2 Pour the mashed grain into a large grain bag to retrieve the sweet wort. Using water slightly hotter than the mash, rinse the grains to collect 20 quarts (19 liters) of extract.

3 Boil the extract with the hops for 1½ hours. Dissolve the malt extract and the sugar in a little hot water and add this during the boil. Also add the Irish moss as directed on the instructions.

4 Turn off the heat. Strain the clear wort into a fermenting bucket and top up to the final quantity with cold water.

5 When cool to room temperature, add the yeast and saccharin tablets. Ferment until the specific gravity falls to 1.015. Rack into 5 quart (4.5 liter) jars or a 25 quart (4.5 liter) fermenter with an airlock. Add gelatin before fitting airlocks.

6 Leave for 7 days before racking the beer from the sediment into a primed pressure barrel. Allow 7 days conditioning before sampling.

Draft Bass

RECIPE BASED ON DRAUGHT BASS BY BASS
WORTHINGTON, BURTON-ON-TRENT

The most famous draft bitter in England, brewed at Burton-on-Trent. A really satisfying brew. Well hopped with a delicate malt flavor.

85

Stage	25 quarts	Original gravity 1.045	25 liters
1	7 lb.	Crushed pale malt	3500 gm
1	8 oz.	Crushed crystal malt	250 gm
1	15 quarts	Water for bitter brewing	15 liters
3	2 oz.	Fuggles hops	60 gm
3, 4, 5	(1 + ½ + ¼) oz.	Goldings hops	(30 + 15 + 10) gm
3	1 tsp.	Irish moss	5 ml
3	1 lb.	Brewing sugar	500 gm
5	2 oz.	Brewer's yeast	60 gm
5	½ oz.	Gelatin	15 gm
6	2 oz.	Dark brown sugar	60 gm

Brewing stages

1 Raise the temperature of the water to 140°F (60°C) and stir in the crushed malts. Stirring continuously, raise the mash temperature to 151°F (66°C). Leave for 1½ hours, occasionally returning the temperature back to this value.

2 Pour the mashed grain into a large grain bag to retrieve the sweet wort. Using water slightly hotter than the mash, rinse the grains to collect 20 quarts (19 liters) of extract.

3 Boil the extract with the Fuggles hops and the first batch of Goldings for 1½ hours. Dissolve the brewing sugar in a little hot water and add this during the boil. Also add the Irish moss as directed on the instructions.

4 Turn off the heat, stir in the second batch of Goldings hops and allow them to soak for 15 minutes. Strain the clear wort into a fermenting bucket and top up to the final quantity with cold water.

5 When cool to room temperature, add the yeast. Ferment 4–5 days until the specific gravity falls to 1.012. Rack into 5 quart (4.5 liter) jars or a 25 quart (24 liter) fermenter fitted with an airlock. Add gelatin and the rest of the dry hops before fitting airlocks.

6 Leave for 7 days before racking the beer from the sediment into a primed pressure barrel. Allow 7 days before sampling.

Brakspear Special Bitter

RECIPE BASED ON SPECIAL BITTER BY
BRAKSPEAR, HENLEY-ON-THAMES.

Delicious, residual sweetness balances this hoppy strong brew.

Stage	25 quarts	Original gravity 1.044	25 liters
1	7 lb.	Crushed pale malt	3500 gm
1	5 oz.	Crushed crystal malt	150 gm
1	8 oz.	Flaked corn	250 gm
1	15 quarts	Water for bitter brewing	15 liters
3	2 oz.	Molasses	60 gm
3	1 oz.	Fuggles hops	30 gm
3, 4, 5	(2 + ½ + ¼) oz.	Goldings hops	(60 + 15 + 10) gm
3	8 oz.	Dark brown sugar	250 gm
3	1 tsp.	Irish moss	5 ml
5	2 oz.	Brewer's yeast	60 gm
5	½ oz.	Gelatin	15 gm
6	2 oz.	Brown sugar	60 gm

Brewing stages

1 Raise the temperature of the water to 140°F (60°C) and stir in the crushed malts and flaked corn. Stirring continuously, raise the mash temperature to 151°F (66°C). Leave for 1½ hours occasionally returning the temperature back to this values

2 Pour the mashed grain into a large grain bag to retrieve the sweet wort. Using water slightly hotter than the mash, rinse the grains to collect 20 quarts (19 liters) of extract.

3 Boil the extract with the Fuggles hops and the first quota of Goldings hops for 1½ hours. Dissolve the dark brown sugar and molasses in a little hot water and add this during the boil. Also add the Irish moss as directed on the instructions.

4 Turn off the heat, stir in the second batch of Goldings hops and allow them to soak for 15 minutes. Strain the clear wort into a fermenting bucket and top up to the final quantity with cold water.

5 When cool to room temperature, add the yeast. Ferment 4–5 days until the specific gravity falls to 1.012. Rack into 5 quart (4.5 liter) jars or a secondary fermentation vessel, fitted with an airlock. Add gelatin and the rest of the dry hops before fitting airlocks.

6 Leave for 7 days before racking the beer from the sediment into a primed pressure barrel. Allow 7 days conditioning before sampling.

Directors Bitter

RECIPE BASED ON DIRECTORS BITTER BY COURAGE, LONDON.

A well-balanced cask-conditioned brew that is rightly claimed as an old fashioned draft bitter and to be alive and kicking.

Stage	25 quarts	Original gravity 1.046	25 liters
1	6 lb.	Crushed pale malt	3000 gm
1	4 oz.	Crushed crystal malt	125 gm
1	15 quarts	Water for bitter brewing	15 liters
1	1 lb.	Barley syrup	500 gm
3	1 tsp.	Irish moss	5 ml
3	2 oz.	Fuggles hops	60 gm
3, 4, 5	(1 + ¼ + ¼) oz.	Goldings hops	(30 + 10 + 10) gm
3, 6	(14 + 2) oz.	Light brown sugar	(450 + 50) gm
5	2 oz.	Brewer's yeast	60 gm
5	½ oz.	Gelatin	15 gm

Brewing stages

1 Raise the temperature of the water to 140°F (60°C) and stir in the crushed malts and barley syrup. Stirring continuously, raise the mash temperature to 151°F (66°C). Leave for 1½ hours occasionally returning the temperature back to this value.

2 Pour the mashed grain into a large grain bag to retrieve the sweet wort. Using water slightly hotter than the mash, rinse the grains to collect 20 quarts (19 liters) of extract.

3 Boil the extract with the Fuggles hops and the first quota of Goldings hops for 1½ hours. Dissolve the first quantity of brown sugar in a little hot water and add this during the boil. Also add the Irish moss as directed on the instructions.

4 Turn off the heat, stir in the second batch of Goldings hops and allow them to soak for 15 minutes. Strain the clear wort into a fermenting bucket and top up to the final quantity with cold water.

5 When cool to room temperature, add the yeast. Ferment 4–5 days until the specific gravity falls to 1.012. Rack into 5 quart (4.5 liter) jars or a 25 quart (24 liter) fermenter fitted with an airlock. Add gelatin and the rest of the dry hops before fitting airlocks.

6 Leave for 7 days before racking the beer from the sediment into a primed pressure barrel. Allow 7 days conditioning before sampling.

Barnsley Bitter

**RECIPE BASED ON BARNSLEY BITTER BY COURAGE,
BARNSLEY (NOW PRODUCED BY ACORN BREWERY).**

This famous beer was once brewed by Oak Well Brewery, which closed in 1974.

Stage	25 quarts	Original gravity 1.037	25 liters
1	5 ¾ lb.	Crushed pale malt	2900 gm
1	3 oz.	Crushed crystal malt	100 gm
1	3 oz.	Flaked corn	100 gm
1	15 quarts	Water for bitter brewing	15 liters
3	8 oz.	Brewing sugar	250 gm
3	2 oz.	Fuggles hops	60 gm
3, 4	(¾ + ¼) oz.	Goldings hops	(25 + 10) gm
3	1 tsp.	Irish moss	5 ml
3	1 tsp.	Brewer's caramel	5 ml
5	2 oz.	Brewer's yeast	60 gm
5	½ oz.	Gelatin	15 gm
6	2 oz.	Brown sugar	60 gm

Brewing stages

1 Raise the temperature of the water to 140°F (60°C) and stir in the crushed malts and flaked corn, Stirring continuously, raise the mash temperature to 151°F (66°C). Leave for 1½ hours occasionally returning the temperature back to this value.

2 Pour the mashed grain into a large grain bag to retrieve the sweet wort. Using water slightly hotter than the mash, rinse the grains to collect 20 quarts (19 liters) of extract.

3 Boil the extract with the Fuggles hops and the first quota of Goldings hops for 1 ½ hours. Dissolve the brewing sugar and caramel in a little hot water and add this during the boil. Also add the Irish moss as directed on the instructions.

4 Turn off the heat, stir in the second batch of Goldings hops and allow them to soak for 15 minutes. Strain the clear wort into a fermenting bucket and top up the final quantity with cold water.

5 When cool to room temperature, add the yeast. Ferment 4–5 days until the specific gravity falls to 1.010. Rack into 5 quart (4.5 liter) jars or a secondary fermentation vessel fitted with an airlock. Add gelatin before fitting airlocks.

6 Leave for 7 days before racking the beer from the sediment into a primed pressure barrel. Allow 7 days conditioning before sampling.

Courage Best Bitter

RECIPE BASED ON BEST BITTER BY COURAGE, BRISTOL.

Hoppy, light golden amber colored brew with a nutty malt flavor.

Stage	25 quarts	Original gravity 1.040	25 liters
1	5¾ lb.	Crushed pale malt	2900 gm
1	4 oz.	Crushed crystal malt	125 gm
1	4 oz.	Flaked barley	125 gm
1	15 quarts	Water for bitter brewing	15 liters
3	1 tsp.	Irish moss	5 ml
3, 6	(14 + 2) oz.	Raw brown sugar	(450 + 50) gm
3, 4	(2½ + ½) oz.	Goldings hops	(75 + 15) gm
3	1 oz.	Northern Brewer hops	30 gm
5	2 oz.	Brewer's yeast	60 gm
5	½ oz.	Gelatin	15 gm

89

Brewing stages

1 Raise the temperature of the water to 140°F (60°C) and stir in the crushed malts and flaked barley. Stirring continuously, raise the mash temperature to 151°F (66°C). Leave for 1½ hours occasionally returning the temperature back to this value.

2 Pour the mashed grain into a large grain bag to retrieve the sweet wort. Using water slightly hotter than the mash, rinse the grains to collect 20 quarts (19 liters) of extract.

3 Boil the extract with the Northern Brewer hops and the first quota of Goldings hops for 1½ hours. Dissolve the main batch of sugar in a little hot water and add this during the boil. Also add the Irish moss as directed on the instructions.

4 Turn off the heat, stir in the second batch of Goldings hops and allow them to soak for 15 minutes. Strain off the clear wort into a fermenting bucket and top up to the final quantity with cold water.

5 When cool to room temperature, add the yeast. Ferment until the specific gravity falls to 1.010. Rack into 5 quart (4.5 liter) jars or a 25 quart (24 liter) fermenter fitted with an airlock. Add gelatin before fitting airlocks.

6 Leave for 7 days before racking the beer from the sediment into a primed beer pressure barrel. Allow 7 days conditioning before sampling.

Davenport Bitter

RECIPE BASED ON BITTER BY DAVENPORT (CARLSBERG-TETLEY, WARRINGTON).

First-class bitter. Light, golden-colored brew, hoppy with a clean palate.

Stage	25 quarts	Original gravity 1.039	25 liters
1	6 lb.	Crushed pale malt	3000 gm
1	3 oz.	Crushed crystal malt	100 gm
1	3 oz.	Crushed wheat malt	100 gm
1	15 quarts	Water for bitter brewing	15 liters
3	1 tsp.	Irish moss	5 ml
3	2 oz.	Molasses	60 gm
3	2½ oz.	Fuggles hops	75 gm
3, 4, 5	(½ + ¼ + ¼) oz.	Goldings hops	(15 + 10 + 10) gm
3, 6	(12 + 2) oz.	Light brown sugar	(400 + 50) gm
5	2 oz.	Brewer's yeast	60 gm
5	½ oz.	Gelatin	15 gm

Brewing stages

1 Raise the temperature of the water to 140°F (60°C) and stir in the crushed malts. Stirring continuously, raise the mash temperature to 151°F (66°C). Leave for 1½ hours, occasionally returning the temperature back to this value.

2 Pour the mashed grain into a large grain bag to retrieve the sweet wort. Using water slightly hotter than the mash, rinse the grains to collect 20 quarts (19 liters) of extract.

3 Boil the extract with the Fuggles hops and the first quota of Goldings hops for 1½ hours. Dissolve the main batch of sugar and molasses in a little hot water and add this during the boil. Also add the Irish moss as directed on the instructions.

4 Turn off the heat, stir in the second batch of Goldings hops and allow them to soak for 15 minutes. Strain the clear wort into a fermenting bucket and top up to the final quantity with cold water.

5 When cool to room temperature, add the yeast. Ferment 4–5 days until the specific gravity falls to 1.010. Rack into 5 quart (4.5 liter) jars or a secondary fermentation vessel fitted with an airlock. Add gelatin and the rest of the dry hops before fitting airlocks.

6 Leave for 7 days before racking the beer from the sediment into primed pressure barrel. Allow 7 days conditioning before sampling.

S. B. A. Bitter

RECIPE BASED ON S. B. A. BITTER BY
DONNINGTON, STOW-ON-THE-WOLD.

Good real ale with a nice hop bite to complement the flavor of malt and
roasted grain.

Stage	25 quarts	Original gravity 1.040	25 liters
1	5½ lb.	Crushed pale malt	2800 gm
1	8 oz.	Flaked barley	250 gm
1	2 oz.	Crushed roast barley	60 gm
1	15 quarts	Water for bitter brewing	15 liters
3	1 tsp.	Irish moss	5 ml
3, 6	(14 + 2) oz.	Raw brown sugar	(450 + 60) gm
3	2 oz.	Fuggles hops	60 gm
3, 4, 5	(1 + ½ + ¼) oz.	Goldings hops	(30 + 15 + 10) gm
5	2 oz.	Brewer's yeast	60 gm
5	½ oz.	Gelatin	15 gm

Brewing Stages

1 Raise the temperature of the water to 140°F (60°C) and stir in the crushed malt and crushed and flaked barley. Stirring continuously, raise the mash temperature to 151°F (66°C). Leave for 1½ hours occasionally returning the temperature back to this value.

2 Pour the mashed grain into a large grain bag to retrieve the sweet wort. Using water slightly hotter than the mash, rinse the grains to collect 20 quarts (19 liters) of extract.

3 Boil the extract with the Fuggles hops and the first quota of Goldings hops for 1½ hours. Dissolve the main batch of sugar in a little hot water and add this during the boil. Also add the Irish moss as directed on the instructions.

4 Turn off the heat, stir in the second batch of Goldings hops and allow them to soak for 15 minutes. Strain the clear wort into a fermenting bucket and top up to the final quantity with cold water.

5 When cool to room temperature, add the yeast. Ferment 4–5 days until the specific gravity falls to 1.010. Rack into 5 quart (4.5 liter) jars or a 25 quart (24 liter) fermenter fitted with an airlock. Add gelatin and the rest of the dry hops before fitting airlocks.

6 Leave for 7 days before racking the beer from the sediment into a primed pressure barrel. Allow 7 days conditioning before sampling.

Royal Oak

RECIPE BASED ON ROYAL OAK BY ELDRIDGE POPE, DORCHESTER.

Excellent draft Pale Ale brewed by these skillful Dorset brewers from a recipe in their brewery museum.

Stage	25 quarts	Original gravity 1.048	25 liters
1	7 lb.	Crushed pale malt	3500 gm
1	14 oz.	Flaked barley	450 gm
1	8 oz.	Crushed crystal malt	250 gm
1	15 quarts	Water for bitter brewing	15 liters
3	1 tsp.	Irish moss	5 ml
3, 6	(12 + 2) oz.	Dark brown sugar	(400 +60) gm
3	2 oz.	Fuggles hops	60 gm
3, 4, 5	(1 + ½+ ¼) oz.	Goldings hops	(30 + 15 + 10) gm
5	2 oz.	Brewer's yeast	60 gm
5	½ oz.	Gelatin	15 gm

Brewing Stages

1 Raise the temperature of the water to 140°F (60°C) and stir in the crushed malts and flaked barley. Stirring continuously, raise the mash temperature to 151°F (66°C). Leave for 1½ hours occasionally returning the temperature back to this value.

2 Pour the mashed grain into a large grain bag to retrieve the sweet wort. Using water slightly hotter than the mash, rinse the grains to collect 20 quarts (19 liters) of extract.

3 Boil the extract with the Fuggles hops and the first quota of Goldings hops for 1½ hours. Dissolve the main batch of sugar in a little hot water and add this during the boil. Also add the Irish moss as directed on the instructions.

4 Turn off the heat, stir in the second batch of Goldings hops and allow them to soak for 15 minutes. Strain off the clear wort into a fermenting bucket and top up to the final quantity with cold water.

5 When cool to room temperature, add the yeast. Ferment until the specific gravity falls to 1.012. Rack into 5 quart (4.5 liter) jars or a secondary fermentation vessel, fitted with an airlock. Add gelatin and the rest of the dry hops before fitting airlocks.

6 Leave for 7 days before racking the beer from the sediment into a primed pressure barrel. Allow 7 days conditioning before sampling.

London Pride

RECIPE BASED ON LONDON PRIDE BY FULLER'S, LONDON.

If I had to select just one beer to drink for the rest of my days, it would have to be London Pride, a classic example of a true English Bitter Beer.

Stage	25 quarts	Original gravity 1.042	25 liters
1	7 lb.	Crushed pale malt	3500 gm
1	8 oz.	Crushed crystal malt	250 gm
1	15 quarts	Water for bitter brewing	15 liters
3	1 tsp.	Irish moss	5 ml
3, 6	(8 + 2) oz.	Raw brown sugar	(250 + 60) gm
3	1 oz.	Fuggles hops	30 gm
3, 4, 5	(2 + ½ + ¼) oz.	Goldings hops	(60 + 15 + 10) gm
5	2 oz.	Brewer's yeast	60 gm
5	½ oz.	Gelatin	15 gm

Brewing Stages

1 Raise the temperature of the water to 140°F (60°C) and stir in the crushed malts. Stirring continuously, raise the mash temperature to 151°F (66°C). Leave for 1½ hours occasionally returning the temperature back to this value.

2 Pour the mashed grain into a large grain bag to retrieve the sweet wort. Using water slightly hotter than the mash, rinse the grains to collect 20 quarts (19 liters) of extract.

3 Boil the extract with the Fuggles hops and the first quota of Goldings hops for 1½ hours. Dissolve the main batch of sugar in a little hot water and add this during the boil. Also add the Irish moss as directed on the instructions.

4 Turn off the heat, stir in the second batch of Goldings hops and allow them to soak for 15 minutes. Strain off the clear wort into a fermenting bucket and top up to the final quantity with cold water.

5 When cool to room temperature, add the yeast. Ferment 4–5 days until the specific gravity falls to 1.012. Rack into 5 quart (4.5 liter) jars or a 25 quart (24 liter) fermenter fitted with an airlock. Add gelatin and the rest of the dry hops before fitting airlocks.

6 Leave for 7 days before racking the beer from the sediment into a primed pressure barrel. Allow 7 days conditioning before sampling.

Horndean Special Bitter (H. S. B.)

RECIPE BASED ON HORNDEAN SPECIAL
BITTER BY GALES, HORNDEAN.

A superb best bitter, well established and respected; an excellent example of true traditional brewing. It is one of the strongest bitters in the United Kingdom and has a distinctive yet delicate sweetness that does not distract from the delightful hop flavor.

Stage	25 quarts	Original gravity 1.051	25 liters
1	8 lb.	Crushed pale malt	4000 gm
1	4 oz.	Crushed crystal malt	125 gm
1	2 oz.	Crushed wheat malt	60 gm
1	15 quarts	Water for bitter brewing	15 liters
3	1 tsp.	Irish moss	5 ml
3	3 oz.	Molasses	100 gm
3	1 oz.	Bramling Cross hops	30 gm
3, 4, 5	(2 + ¾ + ½) oz.	Goldings hops	(60 + 25 + 15) gm
3, 6	(14 + 2) oz.	Dark brown sugar	(450 + 60) gm
5	2 oz.	Brewing yeast	60 gm
5	½ oz.	Gelatin	15 gm
5	5	Saccharin tablets	5

Brewing Stages

1 Raise the temperature of the water to 140°F (60°C) and stir in the crushed malts. Stirring continuously, raise the mash temperature to 151°F (66°C). Leave for 1½ hours occasionally returning the temperature back to this value.

2 Pour the mashed grain into a large grain bag to retrieve the sweet wort. Using water slightly hotter than the mash, rinse the grains to collect 20 quarts (19 liters) of extract.

3 Boil the extract with the Bramling Cross hops and the first quota of Goldings hops for 1½ hours. Dissolve the main batch of sugar and molasses in a little hot water and add this during the boil. Also add the Irish moss as directed on the instructions.

4 Turn off the heat, stir in the second batch of Goldings hops and allow them to soak for 15 minutes. Strain the clear wort into a fermenting bucket and top up to the final quantity with cold water.

5 When cool to room temperature, add the yeast and saccharin tablets. Ferment 4–5 days until the specific gravity falls to 1.015. Rack into 5 quart (4.5 liter) jars or a secondary fermentation vessel fitted with an airlock. Add gelatin and the rest of the dry hops before fitting airlocks.

6 Leave for 7 days before racking the beer from the sediment into a primed pressure barrel. Allow 5 days conditioning before sampling.

Bishops Tipple

RECIPE BASED ON BISHOPS TIPPLE BY GIBBS MEW, SALISBURY.

This is one of the strongest beers to be served on draft in Britain and is a deliciously smooth drink. Initially the extra sweetness takes some getting used to, but after a jar or so you will probably swear it to be "fire and malt nectar," as some of my colleagues do!

Stage	20 quarts	Original gravity 1.066	20 liters
1	7 lb.	Crushed pale malt	3500 gm
1	1 lb.	Crushed crystal malt	500 gm
1	½ oz.	Crushed black malt	15 gm
1	15 quarts	Water for strong ale brewing	15 liters
3	1 tsp.	Irish moss	5 ml
3	1½ lb.	Cane syrup	750 gm
3	2 oz.	Molasses	60 gm
3	3 oz.	Goldings hops	100 gm
5	5	Saccharin tablets	5
5	2 oz.	Brewer's yeast	60 gm
5	½ oz.	Gelatin	15 gm
6	2 oz.	White sugar	60 gm

Brewing Stages

1 Raise the temperature of the water to 140°F (60°C) and stir in the crushed malts. Stirring continuously, raise the mash temperature to 151°F (66°C). Leave for 1½ hours occasionally returning the temperature back to this value.

2 Pour the mashed grain into a large grain bag to retrieve the sweet wort. Using water slightly hotter than the mash, rinse the grains to collect 20 quarts (19 liters) of extract.

3 Boil the extract with the hops for 1½ hours. Dissolve the syrup and molasses in a little hot water and add this during the boil. Also add the Irish moss as directed on the instructions.

4 Turn off the heat. Strain off the clear wort into a fermenting bucket and top up to the final quantity with cold water.

5 When cool to room temperature, add the yeast and saccharin tablets. Ferment until the specific gravity falls to 1.020. Rack into 5 quart (4.5 liter) jars or a 25 quart (24 liter) fermenter fitted with an airlock. Add gelatin before fitting airlocks.

6 Leave for 10 days before racking the beer from the sediment into a primed pressure barrel. Allow 10 days conditioning before sampling.

Abbot Ale

RECIPE BASED ON ABBOT ALE BY GREENE KING, BURY ST. EDMUNDS.

Full bodied, robust, well-opped ale that can be found as a draft bitter or bottled ale. The draft version won the Champion Cup for the best draft bitter in 1968 at the International Brewers' Exhibition.

Stage	25 quarts	Original gravity 1.049	25 liters
1	7½ lb.	Crushed pale malt	3800 gm
1	3 oz.	Crushed crystal malt	100 gm
1	2 oz.	Crushed roast malt	60 gm
1	8 oz.	Flaked corn	250 gm
1	15 quarts	Water for bitter brewing	15 liters
3	1 tsp.	Irish moss	5 ml
3	¾ oz.	Northern Brewer hops	25 gm
3, 4, 5	(3 + ½ + ¼) oz.	Goldings hops	(100 + 15 +10) gm
3, 6	(12 + 2) oz.	Dark brown sugar	(400 + 60) gm
5	2 oz.	Brewer's yeast	60 gm
5	½ oz.	Gelatin	15 gm

Brewing Stages

1 Raise the temperature of the water to 140°F (60°C) and stir in the crushed malts and flaked corn. Stirring continuously raise the mash temperature to 151°F (66°C). Leave for 1½ hours occasionally returning the temperature back to this value.

2 Pour the mashed grain into a large grain bag to retrieve the sweet wort. Using water slightly hotter than the mash, rinse the grains to collect 20 quarts (19 liters) of extract.

3 Boil the extract with the Northern Brewer hops and the first quota of Goldings hops for 1½ hours. Dissolve the main batch of sugar in a little hot water and add this during the boil. Also add the Irish moss as directed on the instructions.

4 Turn off the heat, stir in the second batch of Goldings hops and allow them to soak for 15 minutes. Strain the clear wort into a fermenting bucket and top up to the final quantity with cold water.

5 When cool to room temperature, add the yeast. Ferment 4–5 days until the specific gravity falls to 1.012. Rack into 5 quart (4.5 liter) jars or a secondary fermentation vessel, fitted with an airlock. Add gelatin and the rest of the dry hops before fitting airlocks.

6 Leave for 7 days before racking the beer from the sediment into a primed pressure barrel. Allow 7 days conditioning before sampling.

Badger Best Bitter

RECIPE BASED ON BADGER BEST BITTER BY HALL
& WOODHOUSE, BLANDFORD FORUM.

A beautifully balanced beer and a good example of a best bitter.

Stage	25 quarts	Original gravity 1.042	25 liters
1	5¾ lb.	Crushed pale malt	2900 gm
1	12 oz.	Flaked corn	400 gm
1	4 oz.	Crushed wheat malt	125 gm
1	15 quarts	Water for bitter brewing	15 liters
3	1 tsp.	Irish moss	5 ml
3	2 oz.	Molasses	60 gm
3	1 lb.	Brewing sugar	500 gm
3	2 oz.	Fuggles hops	60 gm
3, 4, 5	(1 + ¼ + ¼) oz.	Goldings hops	(30 +10 + 10) gm
5	2 oz.	Brewer's yeast	60 gm
5	½ oz.	Gelatin	15 gm
6	2 oz.	White sugar	60 gm

Brewing Stages

1 Raise the temperature of the water to 140°F (60°C) and stir in the crushed malts and flaked corn. Stirring continuously, raise the mash temperature to 151°F (66°C). Leave for 1½ hours, occasionally returning the temperature back to this value.

2 Pour the mashed grain into a large grain bag to retrieve the sweet wort. Using water slightly hotter than the mash, rinse the grains to collect 20 quarts (19 liters) of extract.

3 Boil the extract with the Fuggles hops and the first quota of Goldings hops for 1½ hours. Dissolve the brewing sugar and molasses in a little hot water and add this during the boil. Also add the Irish moss as directed on the instructions.

4 Turn off the heat, stir in the second batch of Goldings hops and allow them to soak for 15 minutes. Strain the clear wort into a fermenting bucket and top up to the final quantity with cold water.

5 When cool to room temperature, add the yeast. Ferment 4–5 days until the specific gravity falls to 1.012. Rack into 5 quart (4.5 liter) jars or a 25 quart (24 liter) fermenter fitted with an airlock. Add gelatin and the rest of the dry hops before fitting airlocks.

6 Leave for 7 days before racking the beer from the sediment into a primed pressure barrel. Allow 7 days conditioning before sampling.

Sussex Best Bitter

RECIPE BASED ON SUSSEX BEST BITTER BY HARVEY & SON LTD.

Light, golden brew with a clean palate and a predominate hop flavor

Stage	25 quarts	Original gravity 1.040	25 liters
1	6 lb.	Crushed pale malt	3000 gm
1	8 oz.	Flaked corn	250 gm
1	15 quarts	Water for mild ale brewing	15 liters
3, 6	(8 + 2) oz.	Light brown sugar	(250 + 60) gm
3	2 oz.	Goldings hops	60 gm
3	1 oz.	Northern Brewer hops	30 gm
3	1 tsp.	Irish moss	5 ml
5	2 oz.	Brewer's yeast	60 gm
5	½ oz.	Gelatin	15 gm

Brewing Stages

1 Raise the temperature of the water to 140°F (60°C) and stir in the crushed malt and flaked corn. Stirring continuously, raise the mash temperature up to 151°F (66°C). Leave for 1½ hours occasionally returning the temperature back to this value.

2 Pour the mashed grain into a large grain bag to retrieve the sweet wort. Using water slightly hotter than the mash, rinse the grains to collect 20 quarts (19 liters) of extract.

3 Boil the extract with the hops for 1½ hours. Dissolve the main batch of sugar in a little hot water and add this during the boil. Also add the Irish moss as directed on the instructions.

4 Switch off the heat, strain off the clear wort into a fermenting bucket and top up to the final quantity with cold water.

5 When cool to room temperature, add the yeast. Ferment 4–5 days until the specific gravity falls to 1.010. Rack into 5 quart (4.5 liter) jars or a secondary fermentation vessel, fitted with an airlock. Add gelatin and the rest of the dry hops before fitting airlocks.

6 Leave for 7 days before racking the beer from the sediment into a primed pressure barrel. Allow 7 days conditioning before sampling.

Old Hooky Dark Ale

**RECIPE BASED ON OLD HOOKY DARK ALE
BY HOOK NORTON, BANBURY.**

Very enjoyable well-balanced brew. Like a strong mild and on a par with special bitters. I am sure there is more of a market for this style of beer.

Stage	25 quarts	Original gravity 1.050	25 liters
1	7 lb.	Crushed pale malt	3500 gm
1	3 oz.	Crushed black malt	100 gm
1	10 oz.	Flaked barley	300 gm
1	15 quarts	Water for mild ale brewing	15 liters
3	1 tsp.	Irish moss	5 ml
3	14 oz.	Dark brown sugar	450 gm
3	2 oz.	Fuggles hops	60 gm
3	1 oz.	Bramling Cross hops	30 gm
5	5	Saccharin tablets	5
5	2 oz.	Brewer's yeast	60 gm
5	½ oz.	Gelatin	30 gm
6	2 oz.	Brown sugar	60 gm

Brewing Stages

1 Raise the temperature of the water to 140°F (60°C) and stir in the crushed malts and flakes. Stirring continuously, raise the mash temperature to 151°F (66°C). Leave for 1½ hours, occasionally returning the temperature back to this value.

2 Pour the mashed grain into a large grain bag to retrieve the sweet wort. Using water slightly hotter than the mash, rinse the grains to collect 20 quarts (19 liters) of extract.

3 Boil the extract with the hops for 1½ hours. Dissolve the dark brown sugar in a little hot water and add this during the boil. Also add the Irish moss as directed on the instructions.

4 Turn off the heat. Strain the clear wort into a fermenting bucket and top up to the final quantity with cold water.

5 When cool to room temperature, add the yeast and saccharin tablets. Ferment until the specific gravity falls to 1.014. Rack into 5 quart (4.5 liter) jars or a 25 quart (24 liter) fermenter fitted with an airlock. Add gelatin before fitting airlocks.

6 Leave for 7 days before racking the beer from the sediment into a primed pressure barrel. Allow 7 days conditioning before sampling.

Burton Ale

RECIPE BASED ON BURTON ALE BY IND, COOPE & CO. (CARLSBERG-TETLEY), BURTON-ON-TRENT.

Incredibly smooth ale with a nice flavor from the hops as well as bitterness. Crystal clear, with a fine creamy head, it is the best looking real ale I have seen.

101

Stage	25 quarts	Original gravity 1.048	25 liters
1	6¼ lb.	Crushed pale malt	3175 gm
1	8 oz.	Crushed crystal malt	250 gm
1	15 quarts	Water for bitter brewing	15 liters
3	1 tsp.	Irish moss	5 ml
3	1 lb.	Barley syrup	500 gm
3, 6	(8 + 2) oz.	Dark brown sugar	(500 + 60) gm
3	2 oz.	Molasses	60 gm
3	2 oz.	Fuggles hops	60 gm
3, 4, 5	(1½ + ¼ + ¼) oz.	Goldings hops	(45 + 10 + 10) gm
5	2 oz.	Brewer's yeast	60 gm
5	½ oz.	Gelatin	15 gm
5	5	Saccharin tablets	5

Brewing Stages

1 Raise the temperature of the water to 140°F (60°C) and stir in the crushed malts. Stirring continuously, raise the mash temperature to 151°F (66°C). Leave for 1½ hours, occasionally returning the temperature back to this value.

2 Pour the mashed grain into a large grain bag to retrieve the sweet wort. Using water slightly hotter than the mash, rinse the grains to collect 20 quarts (19 liters) of extract.

3 Boil the extract with the Fuggles hops and the first quota of Goldings hops for 1½ hours. Dissolve the main batch of sugar, molasses and barley syrup in a little hot water and add this during the boil. Also add the Irish moss as directed on the instructions.

4 Turn off the heat, stir in the second batch of Goldings hops and allow them to soak for 15 minutes. Strain the clear wort into a fermenting bucket and top up to the final quantity with cold water.

5 When cool to room temperature, add the yeast. Ferment until the specific gravity falls to 1.012. Rack into 5 quart (4.5 liter) jars or a secondary fermentation vessel fitted with an airlock. Add gelatin and the saccharin tablets and the rest of the dry hops before fitting airlocks.

6 Leave for seven days before racking the beer from the sediment into a primed pressure barrel. Allow seven days conditioning before sampling.

Sussex Pale Ale

RECIPE BASED ON SUSSEX PALE ALE BY KING & BARNES, HORSHAM.

Good, light-bodied bitter with an excellent hop flavor. Sensible gravity for a drinking session because it is a beer you want to stay with.

Stage	25 quarts	Original gravity 1.035	25 liters
1	4¾ lb.	Crushed pale malt	2400 gm
1	1 lb.	Flaked corn	500 gm
1	15 quarts	Water for bitter brewing	15 liters
3	1 tsp.	Irish moss	5 ml
3	6 oz.	Inverted brown sugar (see page 23)	200 gm
3	2 oz.	Fuggles hops	60 gm
3, 4, 5	(½ + ¼ + ¼) oz.	Goldings hops	(15 + 10 + 10) gm
5	2 oz.	Brewer's yeast	60 gm
5	½ oz.	Gelatin	15 gm
6	2 oz.	Brown sugar	60 gm

Brewing Stages

1 Raise the temperature of the water to 140°F (60°C) and stir in the crushed malt and flaked corn. Stirring continuously raise the mash temperature to 151°F (66°C). Leave for 1½ hours, occasionally returning the temperature back to this value.

2 Pour the mashed grain into a large grain bag to retrieve the sweet wort. Using water slightly hotter than the mash, rinse the grains to collect 20 quarts (19 liters) of extract.

3 Boil the extract with the Fuggles hops and the first quota of Goldings hops for 1½ hours. Dissolve the inverted brown sugar in a little hot water and add this during the boil. Also add the Irish moss as directed on the instructions.

4 Turn off the heat, stir in the second batch of Goldings hops and allow them to soak for 15 minutes. Strain the clear wort into a fermenting bucket and top up to the final quantity with cold water.

5 When cool to room temperature, add the yeast. Ferment until the specific gravity falls to 1.010. Rack into 5 quart (4.5 liter) jars or a 25 quart (24 liter) fermenter fitted with an airlock. Add gelatin and the rest of the dry hops before fitting airlocks.

6 Leave for 7 days before racking the beer from the sediment into a primed pressure barrel. Allow 5 days maturation before sampling.

Mild Ale

RECIPE BASED ON MILD ALE BY KING & BARNES, HORSHAM
(NOW OWNED BY HALL AND WOODHOUSE).

Enjoyable, hoppy, mild. A bit like a bitter beer with additional flavor from roasted malts.

Stage	25 quarts	Original gravity 1.033	25 liters
1	4½ lb.	Crushed pale malt	2250 gm
1	5 oz.	Flaked corn	150 gm
1	3 oz.	Crushed black malt	100 gm
1	15 quarts	Water for mild ale brewing	15 liters
3	1 tsp.	Irish moss	5 ml
3	1 lb.	Brewing sugar	500 gm
3	1 tsp.	Brewer's caramel	5 ml
3	½ oz.	W.G.V. or Hallertauer hops	15 gm
3	2 oz.	Fuggles hops	60 gm
5	2 oz.	Brewer's yeast	60 gm
6	2 oz.	Brown sugar	60 gm

Brewing Stages

1 Raise the temperature of the water to 140°F (60°C) and stir in the crushed malts and flaked corn. Stirring continuously, raise the mash temperature up to 151°F (66°C). Leave for 1½ hours, occasionally returning the temperature back to this value.

2 Pour the mashed grain into a large grain bag to retrieve the sweet wort. Using water slightly hotter than the mash, rinse the grains to collect 20 quarts (19 liters) of extract.

3 Boil the extract with the hops for 1½ hours. Dissolve the brewing sugar and caramel in a little hot water and add this during the boil. Also add the Irish moss as directed on the instructions.

4 Turn off the heat. Strain the clear wort into a fermenting bucket and top up to the final quantity with cold water.

5 When cool to room temperature, add the yeast. Ferment 4–5 days until the specific gravity falls to 1.010. Rack into 5 quart (4.5 liter) jars or a secondary fermentation vessel, fitted with an airlock.

6 Leave for 7 days before racking the beer from the sediment into a primed pressure barrel. Allow 7 days conditioning before sampling.

Sussex Old Ale

RECIPE BASED ON SUSSEX OLD ALE BY KING & BARNES, HORSHAM (NOW OWNED BY HALL AND WOODHOUSE).

One of the best old ales I have tasted. Like a full bodied winey strong mild ale.

Stage	25 quarts	Original gravity 1.048	25 liters
1	7¼ lb.	Crushed pale malt	3625 gm
1	5 oz.	Crushed black malt	150 gm
1	15 quarts	Water for old ale brewing	15 liters
3	1 oz.	Molasses	30 gm
3	3 oz.	Fuggles hops	100 gm
3	1 oz.	W.G.V. or Hallertauer hops	30 gm
3	1 tsp.	Irish moss	5 ml
3, 6	(14 + 2) oz.	Dark brown sugar	(450 + 50) gm
5	5	Saccharin tablets	5
5	2 oz.	Brewer's yeast	60 gm
5	½ oz.	Gelatin	15 gm

Brewing Stages

1 Raise the temperature of the water to 140°F (60°C) and stir in the crushed malts. Stirring continuously, raise the mash temperature to 151°F (66°C). Leave for 1½ hours, occasionally returning the temperature back to this value.

2 Pour the mashed grain into a large grain bag to retrieve the sweet wort. Using water slightly hotter than the mash rinse the grains to collect 20 quarts (19 liters) of extract.

3 Boil the extract with the hops for 1½ hours. Dissolve the main batch of sugar and molasses in a little hot water and add this during the boil. Also add the Irish moss as directed on the instructions.

4 Turn off the heat, strain the clear wort into a fermenting bucket and top up to the final quantity with cold water.

5 When cool to room temperature, add the yeast and saccharin tablets. Ferment until the specific gravity falls to 1.012. Rack into 5 quart (4.5 liter) jars or a 25 quart (24 liter) fermenter fitted with an airlock. Add gelatin before fitting airlocks.

6 Leave for 7 days before racking the beer from the sediment into a primed pressure barrel. Allow 7 days conditioning before sampling.

Pedigree Bitter

RECIPE BASED ON PEDIGREE BITTER BY
MARSTON'S, BURTON-ON-TRENT.

Strong, smooth thirst-quenching bitter.

Stage	25 quarts	Original gravity 1.044	25 liters
1	6 lb.	Crushed pale malt	3000 gm
1	15 quarts	Water for bitter brewing	15 liters
3	1 tsp.	Irish moss	5 ml
3	1 lb.	Barley syrup	500 gm
3	1 lb.	Brewing sugar	500 gm
3	1 tsp.	Brewer's caramel	5 ml
3	2½ oz.	Fuggles hops	75 gm
3	1 oz.	Goldings hops	30 gm
5	2 oz.	Brewer's yeast	60 gm
5	½ oz.	Gelatin	15 gm
6	2 oz.	Brown sugar	60 gm

Brewing Stages

1 Raise the temperature of the water to 140°F (60°C) and stir in the crushed malt. Stirring continuously, raise the mash temperature to 151°F (66°C). Leave for 1½ hours, occasionally returning the temperature back to this value.

2 Pour the mashed grain into a large grain bag to retrieve the sweet wort. Using water slightly hotter than the mash, rinse the grains to collect 20 quarts (19 liters) of extract.

3 Boil the extract with the hops for 1½ hours. Dissolve the barley syrup, caramel and the brewing sugar in a little hot water and add this during the boil. Also add the Irish moss as directed on the instructions.

4 Turn off the heat, strain the clear wort into a fermenting bucket and top up to the final quantity with cold water.

5 When cool to room temperature, add the yeast. Ferment 4–5 days until the specific gravity falls to 1.012. Rack into 5 quart (4.5 liter) jars or a secondary fermentation vessel fitted with an airlock. Add gelatin before fitting airlocks.

6 Leave for 7 days before racking the beer from the sediment into a primed pressure barrel. Allow 7 days conditioning before sampling.

D. P. A. Bitter

RECIPE BASED ON D. P. A. BITTER BY MITCHELLS & BUTLERS (BASS).

This bitter, Dunkirk Pale Ale, is often served as a light, mild ale and called Derby Pale Ale!

Stage	25 quarts	Original gravity 1.033	25 liters
1	4¼ lb.	Crushed pale malt	2200 gm
1	10 oz.	Flaked corn	300 gm
1	12.5 quarts	Water for light ale brewing	12 liters
3	1 tsp.	Irish moss	5 ml
3, 6	(14 + 2) oz.	Raw brown sugar	(450 + 60) gm
3	2 oz.	Fuggles hops	60 gm
5	2 oz.	Brewer's yeast	60 gm
5	½ oz.	Gelatin	15 gm

Brewing Stages

1 Raise the temperature of the water to 140°F (60°C) and stir in the crushed malt and flaked corn. Stirring continuously, raise the mash temperature to 151°F (66°C). Leave for 1½ hours, occasionally returning the temperature back to this value.

2 Pour the mashed grain into a large grain bag to retrieve the sweet wort. Using water slightly hotter than the mash, rinse the grains to collect 20 quarts (19 liters) of extract.

3 Boil the extract with the hops for 1½ hours. Dissolve the main batch of sugar in a little hot water and add this during the boil. Also add the Irish moss as directed on the instructions.

4 Turn off the heat, strain the clear wort into a fermenting bucket and top up to the final quantity with cold water.

5 When cool to room temperature, add the yeast. Ferment 4–5 days until the specific gravity falls to 1.010. Rack into 5 quart (4.5 liter) jars or a 25 quart (24 liter) fermenter fitted with an airlock. Add gelatin before fitting airlocks.

6 Leave for 7 days before racking the beer from the sediment into a primed pressure barrel. Allow 7 days conditioning before sampling.

Morland Best Bitter

RECIPE BASED ON BEST BITTER BY MORLAND, ABINGDON (NOW OWNED BY GREENE KING).

Lovely hop flavor blended with real expertise in this full, malty brew. Eventually replaced by an improved beer called Old Masters.

107

Stage	25 quarts	Original gravity 1.043	25 liters
1	7 lb.	Crushed pale malt	3500 gm
1	4 oz.	Crushed crystal malt	125 gm
1	15 quarts	Water for bitter brewing	15 liters
3	1 tsp.	Irish moss	5 ml
3	½ oz.	Fuggles hops	15 gm
3	½ oz.	Bramling Cross hops	15 gm
3, 4, 5	(2 + ½ + ¼) oz.	East Kent Goldings hops	(60 + 15 +10) gm
3, 6	(12 + 2) oz.	Dark brown sugar	(400 + 50) gm
5	2 oz.	Brewer's yeast	60 gm
5	½ oz.	Gelatin	15 gm

Brewing Stages

1 Raise the temperature of the water to 140°F (60°C) and stir in the crushed malts. Stirring continuously, raise the mash temperature to 151°F (66°C). Leave for 1½ hours, occasionally returning the temperature back to this value.

2 Pour the mashed grain into a large grain bag to retrieve the sweet wort. Using water slightly hotter than the mash, rinse the grains to collect 20 quarts (19 liters) of extract.

3 Boil the extract with the Fuggles and Bramling Cross hops and the first quota of East Kent Goldings hops for 1½ hours. Dissolve the main batch of sugar in a little hot water and add this during the boil. Also add the Irish moss as directed on the instructions.

4 Turn off the heat, stir in the second batch of East Kent Goldings hops and allow them to soak for 15 minutes. Strain the clear wort into a fermenting bucket and top up to the final quantity with cold water.

5 When cool to room temperature, add the yeast. Ferment 4–5 days until the specific gravity falls to 1.012. Rack into 5 quart (4.5 liter) jars or a secondary fermentation vessel fitted with an airlock. Add gelatin and the rest of the dry hops before fitting airlocks.

6 Leave for 7 days before racking the beer from the sediment into a primed pressure barrel. Allow 7 days conditioning before sampling.

Mild Ale

**RECIPE BASED ON MILD ALE BY MORLAND,
ABINGDON (NOW OWNED BY GREENE KING).**

I was very impressed with this brew. A particularly good example of mild ale. Called "Ale" locally. Production stopped some time ago, and it was replaced by a new mild beer, Revival Mild.

Stage	25 quarts	Original gravity 1.033	25 liters
1	5 lb.	Crushed pale malt	2500 gm
1	4 oz.	Crushed roast barley	125 gm
1	12.5 quarts	Water for mild ale brewing	12 liters
3	1 tsp.	Irish moss	5 ml
3	2 oz.	Fuggles hops	60 gm
3, 6	(12 + 2) oz.	Dark brown sugar	(400 + 50) gm
5	2 oz.	Brewer's yeast	60 gm

Brewing Stages

1 Raise the temperature of the water to 140°F (60°C) and stir in the crushed malt and barley. Stirring continuously, raise the mash temperature up to 151°F (66°C). Leave for 1½ hours, occasionally returning the temperature back to this value.

2 Pour the mashed grain into a large grain bag to retrieve the sweet wort. Using water slightly hotter than the mash, rinse the grains to collect 20 quarts (19 liters) of extract.

3 Boil the extract with the hops for 1½ hours. Dissolve the main batch of sugar in a little hot water and add this during the boil. Also add the Irish moss as directed on the instructions.

4 Turn off the heat, strain the clear wort into a fermenting bucket and top up to the final quantity with cold water.

5 When cool to room temperature, add the yeast. Ferment 4–5 days until the specific gravity falls to 1.010. Rack into 5 quart (4.5 liter) jars or a 25 quart (24 liter) fermenter fitted with an airlock.

6 Leave for 7 days before racking the beer from the sediment into a primed pressure barrel. Allow 7 days conditioning before sampling.

Varsity Bitter

RECIPE BASED ON VARSITY BITTER BY MORRELL, OXFORD.

Good best bitter; well balanced and malty.

Stage	25 quarts	Original gravity 1.041	25 liters
1	5¾ lb.	Crushed pale malt	2900 gm
1	8 oz.	Crushed crystal malt	250 gm
1	1 oz.	Crushed roasted barley	30 gm
1	15 quarts	Water for bitter brewing	15 liters
3	1 tsp.	Irish moss	5 ml
3, 6	(14 + 2) oz.	Raw brown sugar	(450 + 60) gm
3	3 oz.	Fuggles hops	100 gm
5	2 oz.	Brewer's yeast	60 gm
5	½ oz.	Gelatin	15 gm

Brewing Stages

1 Raise the temperature of the water to 140°F (60°C) and stir in the crushed malts and barley. Stirring continuously, raise the mash temperature to 151°F (66°C). Leave for 1½ hours, occasionally returning the temperature back to this value.

2 Pour the mashed grain into a large grain bag to retrieve the sweet wort. Using water slightly hotter than the mash, rinse the grains to collect 20 quarts (19 liters) of extract.

3 Boil the extract with the hops for 1½ hours. Dissolve the main batch of sugar in a little hot water and add this during the boil. Also add the Irish moss as directed on the instructions.

4 Turn off the heat, strain the clear wort into a fermenting bucket and top up to the final quantity with cold water.

5 When cool to room temperature, add the yeast. Ferment 4–5 days until the specific gravity falls to 1.010. Rack into 5 quart (4.5 liter) jars or a 25 quart (24 liter) fermenter fitted with an airlock. Add gelatin before fitting airlocks.

6 Leave for 7 days before racking the beer from the sediment into a primed pressure barrel. Allow 7 days conditioning before sampling.

E. G. Bitter

RECIPE BASED ON E. G. BITTER BY PAINES, ST. NEOTS.

Eynesbury Giant or Extra Gravity was a full-bodied sweetish malty brew with a beautiful, sugary bouquet.

Stage	25 quarts	Original gravity 1.049	25 liters
1	7¼ lb.	Crushed pale malt	3625 gm
1	15 quarts	Water for bitter brewing	15 liters
3	1 lb.	Light brown sugar	500 gm
3	1 tsp.	Irish moss	5 ml
3	2 oz.	Fuggles hops	60 gm
3	1½ oz.	Goldings hops	45 gm
3, 6	(2 + 1) oz.	Black treacle	(60 + 30) gm
5	5	Saccharin tablets	5
5	2 oz.	Brewer's yeast	60 gm
5	½ oz.	Gelatin	15 gm
6	1 oz.	Brown sugar	30 gm

Brewing Stages

1 Raise the temperature of the water to 140°F (60°C) and stir in the crushed malt. Stirring continuously, raise the mash temperature to 151°F (66°C). Leave for 1½ hours, occasionally returning the temperature back to this value.

2 Pour the mashed grain into a large grain bag to retrieve the sweet wort. Using water slightly hotter than the mash, rinse the grains to collect 20 quarts (19 liters) of extract.

3 Boil the extract with the hops for 1½ hours. Dissolve the light brown sugar and treacle in a little hot water and add this during the boil. Also add the Irish moss as directed on the instructions,

4 Turn off the heat, strain the clear wort into a fermenting bucket and top up to the final quantity with cold water.

5 When cool to room temperature, add the yeast and saccharin tablets. Ferment 4–5 days until the specific gravity falls to 1.012. Rack into 5 quart (4.5 liter) jars or a secondary fermentation vessel fitted with an airlock. Add gelatin before fitting airlocks.

6 Leave for 7 days before racking the beer from the sediment into a primed pressure barrel. Allow 7 days conditioning before sampling.

Draft I. P. A.

RECIPE BASED ON DRAUGHT I. P. A. BY PALMERS, BRIDPORT.

A most impressive pale ale with a first class hop flavor. Deserves far more recognition.

Stage	25 quarts	Original gravity 1.040	25 liters
1	6 lb.	Crushed pale malt	3000 gm
1	2 oz.	Crushed roasted barley	60 gm
1	15 quarts	Water for bitter brewing	15 liters
3	1 tsp.	Irish moss	5 ml
3	1 lb.	Brewing sugar	500 gm
3	1 oz.	Molasses	30 gm
3	1 ¼ oz.	Fuggles hops	40 gm
3, 4, 5	(2 + ¼ + ¼) oz.	Goldings hops	(60 + 10 +10) gm
5	2 oz.	Brewer's yeast	60 gm
5	½ oz.	Gelatin	15 gm
6	2 oz.	Brown sugar	60 gm

Brewing Stages

1 Raise the temperature of the water to 140°F (60°C) and stir in the crushed malt and barley. Stirring continuously, raise the mash temperature to 151°F (66°C). Leave for 1½ hours, occasionally returning the temperature back to this value.

2 Pour the mashed grain into a large grain bag to retrieve the sweet wort. Using water slightly hotter than the mash, rinse the grains to collect 20 quarts (19 liters) of extract.

3 Boil the extract with the Fuggles hops and the first quota of Goldings hops for 1½ hours. Dissolve the brewing sugar and molasses in a little hot water and add this during the boil. Also add the Irish moss as directed on the instructions.

4 Turn off the heat, stir in the second batch of Goldings hops and allow them to soak for 15 minutes. Strain the clear wort into a fermenting bucket and top up to the final quantity with cold water.

5 When cool to room temperature, add the yeast. Ferment 4–5 days until the specific gravity falls to 1.010. Rack into 5 quart (4.5 liter) jars or a 25 quart (24 liter) fermenter fitted with an airlock. Add gelatin and the rest of the dry hops before fitting airlocks.

6 Leave for 7 days before racking the beer from the sediment into a primed pressure barrel. Allow 7 days conditioning before sampling.

County Bitter

RECIPE BASED ON COUNTY BITTER BY RUDDLES, OAKHAM (NOW OWNED BY GREENE KING).

A robust bitter packed with the flavor of malt and hops.

Stage	25 quarts	Original gravity 1.050	25 liters
1	7¾ lb.	Crushed pale malt	3875 gm
1	8 oz.	Crushed crystal malt	250 gm
1	15 quarts	Water for bitter brewing	15 liters
3	1 tsp.	Irish moss	5 ml
3	1 lb.	Brewing sugar	500 gm
3	1 oz.	Molasses	30 gm
3	2 tsp.	Brewer's caramel	10 ml
3	2 oz.	Fuggles hops	60 gm
3, 4	(1½ + ½) oz.	W.G.V. or Hallertauer hops	(45 + 15) gm
5	2 oz.	Brewer's yeast	60 gm
5	½ oz.	Gelatin	15 gm
6	2 oz.	Brown sugar	60 gm

Brewing Stages

1 Raise the temperature of the water to 140°F (60°C) and stir in the crushed malts. Stirring continuously, raise the mash temperature to 151°F (66°C). Leave for 1½ hours, occasionally returning the temperature back to this value.

2 Pour the mashed grain into a large grain bag to retrieve the sweet wort. Using water slightly hotter than the mash, rinse the grains to collect 20 quarts (19 liters) of extract.

3 Boil the extract with the Fuggles hops and the first quota of W.G.V. hops for 1½ hours. Dissolve the brewing sugar, molasses and caramel in a little hot water and add this during the boil. Also add the Irish moss as directed on the instructions.

4 Turn off the heat, stir in the second batch of W.G.V. hops and allow them to soak for 15 minutes. Strain the clear wort into a fermenting bucket and top up to the final quantity with cold water.

5 When cool to room temperature, add the yeast. Ferment 4–5 days until the specific gravity falls to 1.015. Rack into 5 quart (4.5 liter) jars or a secondary fermentation vessel fitted with an airlock. Add gelatin before fitting airlocks.

6 Leave for 7 days before racking the beer from the sediment into a primed pressure barrel. Allow 7 days conditioning before sampling.

Old Brewery Bitter

**RECIPE BASED ON OLD BREWERY BITTER
BY SAMUEL SMITH, TADCASTER.**

Strong bitter with a light golden color and unusual, but very pleasant, cask malt flavor.

Stage	25 quarts	Original gravity 1.040	25 liters
1	6 lb.	Crushed pale malt	3000 gm
1	8 oz.	Torrefied barley	250 gm
1	6 oz.	Crushed crystal malt	200 gm
1	15 quarts	Water for bitter brewing	15 liters
3	1 tsp.	Irish moss	5 ml
3	8 oz.	Brewing sugar	250 gm
3	2 oz.	Molasses	60 gm
3	2½ oz.	Fuggles hops	75 gm
3	½ oz.	Goldings hops	15 gm
5	2 oz.	Brewer's yeast	60 gm
5	½ oz.	Gelatin	15 gm
6	2 oz.	Brown sugar	60 gm

Brewing Stages

1 Raise the temperature of the water to 140°F (60°C) and stir in the crushed malts and grain. Stirring continuously, raise the mash temperature to 151°F (66°C). Leave for 1½ hours, occasionally returning the temperature back to this value.

2 Pour mashed grain into a large grain bag to retrieve the sweet wort. Using water slightly hotter than the mash, rinse the grains to collect 20 quarts (19 liters) of extract.

3 Boil the extract with the hops for 1½ hours. Dissolve the main batch of sugar and molasses in a little hot water and add this during the boil. Also add the Irish moss as directed on the instructions.

4 Turn off the heat, strain the clear wort into a fermenting bucket and top up to the final quantity with cold water.

5 When cool to room temperature, add the yeast. Ferment 4–5 days until the specific gravity falls to 1.010. Rack into 5 quart (4.5 liter) jars or a 25 quart (24 liter) fermenter fitted with an airlock. Add gelatin before fitting airlocks.

6 Leave for 7 days before racking the beer from the sediment into a primed pressure barrel. Allow 7 days conditioning before sampling.

Shepherd Neame Best Bitter

RECIPE BASED ON BEST BITTER BY SHEPHERD NEAME, FAVERSHAM.

Smoky malt flavor makes it the most easily recognized bitter in the United Kingdom, as well as being one of the best.

Stage	25 quarts	Original gravity 1.040	25 liters
1	6 lb.	Crushed pale malt	3000 gm
1	6 oz.	Flaked corn	200 gm
1	6 oz.	Crushed amber malt	200 gm
1	15 quarts	Water for bitter brewing	15 liters
3	1 tsp.	Irish moss	5 ml
3	8 oz.	Dark brown sugar	250 gm
3	1 oz.	W.G.V. or Hallertauer hops	30 gm
3, 4, 5	(1 + ¼ + ¼) oz.	Goldings hops	(60 + 10 + 10) gm
5	2 oz.	Brewer's yeast	60 gm
5	½ oz.	Gelatin	15 gm
6	2 oz.	Brown sugar	60 gm

Brewing Stages

1 Raise the temperature of the water to 140°F (60°C) and stir in the crushed malts and flaked corn. Stirring continuously, raise the mash temperature to 151°F (66°C). Leave for 1½ hours, occasionally returning the temperature back to this value.

2 Pour the mashed grain into a large grain bag to retrieve the sweet wort. Using water slightly hotter than the mash, rinse the grains to collect 20 quarts (19 liters) of extract.

3 Boil the extract with the W.G.V. hops and the first quota of Goldings hops for 1½ hours. Dissolve the dark brown sugar in a little hot water and add this during the boil. Also add the Irish moss as directed on the instructions.

4 Turn off the heat, stir in the second batch of Goldings hops and allow them to soak for 15 minutes. Strain the clear wort into a fermenting bucket and top up to the final quantity with cold water.

5 When cool to room temperature, add the yeast. Ferment 4–5 days until the specific gravity falls to 1.010. Rack into 5 quart (4.5 liter) jars or a secondary fermentation vessel, fitted with an airlock. Add gelatin and the rest of the dry hops before fitting airlocks.

6 Leave for 7 days before racking the beer from the sediment into a primed pressure barrel. Allow 7 days conditioning before sampling.

Tetley Bitter

RECIPE BASED ON BITTER BY TETLEY, LEEDS.

A creamy, smooth, well-balanced bitter that deserves its loyal following.

Stage	25 quarts	Original gravity 1.036	25 liters
1	4¾ lb.	Crushed pale malt	2400 gm
1	6 oz.	Crushed crystal malt	200 gm
1	6 oz.	Crushed wheat malt	200 gm
1	15 quarts	Water for bitter brewing	15 liters
3	1 tsp.	Irish moss	5 ml
3	1 lb.	Light brown sugar	500 gm
3	2½ oz.	Fuggles hops	75 gm
3	½ oz.	Bramling Cross hops	15 gm
5	2 oz.	Brewer's yeast	60 gm
5	½ oz.	Gelatin	15 gm
6	1 oz.	Brown sugar	30 gm

Brewing Stages

1 Raise the temperature of the water to 140°F (60°C) and stir in the crushed malts. Stirring continuously, raise the mash temperature to 151°F (66°C). Leave for 1½ hours, occasionally returning the temperature back to this value.

2 Pour the mashed grain into a large grain bag to retrieve the sweet wort. Using water slightly hotter than the mash, rinse the grains to collect 20 quarts (19 liters) of extract.

3 Boil the extract with the hops for 1½ hours. Dissolve the light brown sugar in a little hot water and add this during the boil. Also add the Irish moss as directed on the instructions.

4 Turn off the heat, strain the clear wort into a fermenting bucket and top up to the final quantity with cold water.

5 When cool to room temperature, add the yeast. Ferment 4–5 days until the specific gravity falls to 1.010. Rack into 5 quart (4.5 liter) jars or a 25 quart (24 liter) fermenter fitted with an airlock. Add gelatin before fitting airlocks.

6 Leave for 7 days before racking the beer from the sediment into a primed pressure barrel. Allow 7 days conditioning before sampling.

Old Peculier

RECIPE BASED ON OLD PECULIER BY THEAKSTONS, MASHAM AND NEWCASTLE.

Aptly named, this brew is unusual, very distinct, but pleasantly peculiar. The dark brew owes much of its charm to the bouquet, flavor and after taste of the priming sugars. My notes record it as one of the best dark draft beers I have tasted and a good example of an old-fashioned ale.

Stage	25 quarts	6% Alcohol	25 liters
1	15 quarts	Water for brown ale brewing	15 liters
1	4 lb.	Dark malt extract	2000 gm
1	8 oz.	Crushed roast barley	250 gm
1	8 oz.	Crushed crystal malt	250 gm
1	2 lb.	Dark brown sugar	1000 gm
1	2 oz.	Fuggles hops	60 gm
2	5	Saccharin tablets	5
2	2 oz.	Brewer's yeast	60 gm
3	3 oz.	Black treacle	100 gm

Brewing Stages

1 Boil the malt extract, malt grains and hops in water for 45 minutes. Carefully strain the wort from the hops and malt and barley into a fermenting bucket. Rinse the spent grains and hops with two pots of hot water. Dissolve the dark brown sugar in hot water and add this to the bucket. Top up to the final quantity with cold water.

2 When cool to room temperature, add the yeast and saccharin tablets. Ferment until the activity abates. Rack into secondary fermentation vessels and keep under airlock protection for another 7 days.

3 Rack the beer from the sediment into a barrel primed with treacle. Allow 7 days conditioning before sampling.

Theakstons Best Bitter

RECIPE BASED ON BEST BITTER BY THEAKSTONS,
MASHAM AND NEWCASTLE.

A good real ale. Very light colored but with ample malt body to balance the
hops. If you can get some of the brewery yeast, so much the better, as this ale
benefits from the slight yeast flavor.

Stage	25 quarts	Original gravity 1.038	25 liters
1	5½ lb.	Crushed pale malt	2800 gm
1	12 oz.	Flaked corn	400 gm
1	15 quarts	Water for bitter brewing	15 liters
3	1 tsp.	Irish moss	5 ml
3	6 oz.	Raw brown sugar	200 gm
3	2 oz.	Fuggles hops	60 gm
3, 4, 5	(1 + ½ + ¼) oz.	Goldings hops	(30 + 15 + 10) gm
5	2 oz.	Brewing yeast	60 gm
5	½ oz.	Gelatin	15 gm
6	2 oz.	Dark brown sugar	60 gm

Brewing Stages

1 Raise the temperature of the water to 140°F (60°C) and stir in the crushed malt and flaked corn. Stirring continuously, raise the mash temperature to 151°F (66°C). Leave for 1½ hours, occasionally returning the temperature back to this value.

2 Pour the mashed grain into a large grain bag to retrieve the sweet wort. Using water slightly hotter than the mash, rinse the grains to collect 20 quarts (19 liters) of extract.

3 Boil the extract with the Fuggles hops and the first quota of Goldings hops for 1½ hours. Dissolve the raw brown sugar in a little hot water and add this during the boil. Also add the Irish moss as directed on the instructions.

4 Turn off the heat, stir in the second batch of Goldings hops and allow them to soak for 15 minutes. Strain the clear wort into a fermenting bucket and top up to the final quantity with cold water.

5 When cool to room temperature, add the yeast. Ferment 4–5 days until the specific gravity falls to 1.010. Rack into 5 quart (4.5 liter) jars or a 25 quart (24 liter) fermenter with an airlock. Add gelatin and the rest of the dry hops before fitting airlocks.

6 Leave for 7 days before racking the beer from the sediment into a primed pressure barrel. Allow 7 days conditioning before sampling.

Tolly Cobbold Bitter

RECIPE BASED ON BITTER BY TOLLY COBBOLD, IPSWICH.

Full-flavored bitter for its gravity, smooth and very tasty.

Stage	25 quarts	Original gravity 1.035	25 liters
1, 2	12.5 quarts	Water for bitter brewing	12 liters
1	1 lb.	Wheat flour	500 gm
2	4¾ lb.	Crushed pale malt	2400 gm
2	4 oz.	Crushed crystal malt	125 gm
4	1 tsp.	Irish moss	5 ml
4	2 oz.	Fuggles hops	60 gm
4, 5	(¾ + ¼) oz.	Goldings hops	(25 + 10) gm
4, 7	(8 + 2) oz.	Dark brown sugar	(250 + 50) gm
6	2 oz.	Brewer's yeast	60 gm
6	½ oz.	Gelatin	15 gm

Brewing Stages

1 Mix the wheat flour as a paste before thoroughly dissolving it in the cold water for mashing.

2 Raise the temperature of the water to 140°F (60°C) and stir in the crushed malts. Stirring continuously, raise the mash temperature to 151°F (66°C). Leave for 1½ hours occasionally returning the temperature back to this value.

3 Pour the mashed grain into a large grain bag to retrieve the sweet wort. Using water slightly hotter than the mash, rinse the grains to collect 20 quarts (19 liters) of extract.

4 Boil the extract with the Fuggles hops and the first quota of Goldings hops for 1½ hours. Dissolve the main batch of sugar in a little hot water and add this during the boil. Also add the Irish moss as directed on the instructions.

5 Turn off the heat, stir in the second batch of Goldings hops and allow them to soak for 15 minutes. Strain the clear wort into a fermenting bucket and top up to the final quantity with cold water.

6 When cool to room temperature, add the yeast. Ferment 4–5 days until the specific gravity falls to 1.010. Rack into 5 quart (4.5 liter) jars or a secondary fermentation vessel, fitted with an airlock. Add gelatin before fitting airlocks.

7 Leave for 7 days before racking the beer from the sediment into a primed pressure barrel. Allow 7 days conditioning before sampling.

Usher's P. A.

RECIPE BASED ON USHER'S P. A. BY USHER, TROWBRIDGE.

A light, refreshing bitter.

Stage	25 quarts	Original gravity 1.032	25 liters
1	4 lb. 8 oz.	Crushed pale malt	2250 gm
1	14 oz.	Flaked corn	450 gm
1	12.5 quarts	Water for bitter brewing	12 liters
3	1 tsp.	Irish moss	5 ml
3	12 oz.	Brewing sugar	400 gm
3	3 oz.	Fuggles hops	100 gm
5	2 oz.	Brewer's yeast	60 gm
5	½ oz.	Gelatin	15 gm
6	2 oz.	Brown sugar	60 gm

Brewing Stages

1 Raise the temperature of the water to 140°F (60°C) and stir in the crushed malts and flaked corn. Stirring continuously, raise the mash temperature to 151°F (66°C). Leave for 1½ hours, occasionally returning the temperature back to this value.

2 Pour the mashed grain into a large grain bag to retrieve the sweet wort. Using water slightly hotter than the mash, rinse the grains to collect 20 quarts (19 liters) of extract.

3 Boil the extract with the hops for 1½ hours. Dissolve the brewing and brown sugar in a little hot water and add this during the boil. Also add the Irish moss as directed on the instructions.

4 Turn off the heat, strain the clear wort into a fermenting bucket and top up to the final quantity with cold water.

5 When cool to room temperature, add the yeast. Ferment 4–5 days until the specific gravity falls to 1.010. Rack into 5 quart (4.5 liter) jars or a 25 quart (24 liter) fermenter fitted with an airlock. Add gelatin before fitting airlocks.

6 Leave for 7 days before racking the beer from the sediment into a primed pressure barrel. Allow 7 days conditioning before sampling.

6X Bitter

RECIPE BASED ON 6X BITTER BY WADWORTH, DEVIZES.

A nice light-colored, hoppy brew.

Stage	25 quarts	Original gravity 1.040	25 liters
1	5¼ lb.	Crushed pale malt	2700 gm
1	12 oz.	Flaked corn	400 gm
1	8 oz.	Crushed crystal malt	250 gm
1	15 quarts	Water for bitter brewing	15 liters
3	1 tsp.	Irish moss	5 ml
3	10 oz.	Brewing sugar	300 gm
3	2 oz.	Goldings hops	60 gm
3	1 oz.	Bramling Cross hops	30 gm
5	2 oz.	Brewer's yeast	60 gm
5	½ oz.	Gelatin	15 gm
6	2 oz.	Brown sugar	60 gm

Brewing Stages

1 Raise the temperature of the water to 140°F (60°C) and stir in the crushed malts and flaked corn. Stirring continuously, raise the mash temperature to 151°F (66°C). Leave for 1½ hours, occasionally returning the temperature back to this value.

2 Pour the mashed grain into a large grain bag to retrieve the sweet wort. Using water slightly hotter than the mash, rinse the grains to collect 20 quarts (19 liters) of extract.

3 Boil the extract with the hops for 1½ hours. Dissolve the brewing sugar in a little hot water and add this during the boil. Also add the Irish moss as directed on the instructions.

4 Turn off the heat, strain the clear wort into a fermenting bucket and top up to the final quantity with cold water.

5 When cool to room temperature, add the yeast. Ferment 4–5 days until the specific gravity falls to 1.010. Rack into 5 quart (4.5 liter) jars or a secondary fermentation vessel fitted with an airlock. Add gelatin before fitting airlocks.

6 Leave for 7 days before racking the beer from the sediment into a primed pressure barrel. Allow 7 days conditioning before sampling.

Old Timer

RECIPE BASED ON OLD TIMER BY WADWORTH, DEVIZES.

Generous, malty brew that is deceptively strong—as I found to my pleasure!

Stage	25 quarts	Original gravity 1.054	25 liters
1	7½ lb.	Crushed pale malt	3750 gm
1	4 oz.	Crushed crystal malt	125 gm
1	12 oz.	Flaked barley	400 gm
1	15 quarts	Water for bitter brewing	15 liters
3	1 tsp.	Irish moss	5 ml
3	1 lb.	Brewing sugar	500 gm
3	2 oz.	Fuggles hops	60 gm
3, 4, 5	(1 + ½ + ¼) oz.	Goldings hops	(30 + 15 + 10) gm
3, 6	(6 + 2) oz.	Dark brown sugar	(200 + 50) gm
5	2 oz.	Brewer's yeast	60 gm
5	½ oz.	Gelatin	15 gm

Brewing Stages

1 Raise the temperature of the water to 140°F (60°C) and stir in the crushed malts and flaked barley. Stirring continuously, raise the mash temperature up to 151°F (66°C). Leave for 1½ hours, occasionally returning the temperature back to this value.

2 Pour the mashed grain into a large grain bag to retrieve the sweet wort. Using water slightly hotter than the mash, rinse the grains to collect 20 quarts (19 liters) of extract.

3 Boil the extract with the Fuggles hops and the first quota of Goldings hops for 1½ hours. Dissolve the brewing and brown sugar in a little hot water and add this during the boil. Also add the Irish moss as directed on the instructions.

4 Turn off the heat, stir in the second batch of Goldings hops and allow them to soak for 15 minutes. Strain the clear wort into a fermenting bucket and top up to the final quantity with cold water.

5 When cool to room temperature, add the yeast. Ferment 4–5 days until the specific gravity falls to 1.015. Rack into 5 quart (4.5 liter) jars or a 25 quart (24 liter) fermenter fitted with an airlock. Add gelatin and the rest of the dry hops before fitting airlocks.

6 Leave for 7 days before racking the beer from the sediment into a primed pressure barrel. Allow 7 days conditioning before sampling.

Yorkshire Bitter

RECIPE BASED ON YORKSHIRE BITTER
BY WEBSTER'S (COURAGE), HALIFAX.

Highly individual brew. Full bodied, sweetish, not too malty,

but generously hopped.

Stage	25 quarts	Original gravity 1.038	25 liters
1	5½ lb.	Crushed pale malt	2800 gm
1	5 oz.	Crushed crystal malt	150 gm
1	5 oz.	Crushed wheat malt	150 gm
1	15 quarts	Water for bitter brewing	15 liters
3	1 tsp.	Irish moss	5 ml
3	1 lb.	Brewing sugar	500 gm
3	3 oz.	Fuggles hops	100 gm
4	½ oz.	Bramling Cross hops	15 gm
5	2 oz.	Brewer's yeast	60 gm
5	½ oz.	Gelatin	15 gm
6	2 oz.	Brown sugar	60 gm

Brewing Stages

1 Raise the temperature of the water to 140°F (60°C) and stir in the crushed malts. Stirring continuously, raise the mash temperature to 151°F (66°C). Leave for 1½ hours, occasionally returning the temperature back to this value.

2 Pour the mashed grain into a large grain bag to retrieve the sweet wort. Using water slightly hotter than the mash, rinse the grains to collect 20 quarts (19 liters) of extract.

3 Boil the extract with the Fuggles hops for 1½ hours. Dissolve the brewing sugar in a little hot water and add this during the boil. Also add the Irish moss as directed on the instructions.

4 Turn off the heat, stir in the Bramling Cross hops and allow them to soak for 15 minutes. Strain the clear wort into a fermenting bucket and top up to the final quantity with cold water.

5 When cool to room temperature, add the yeast. Ferment 4–5 days until the specific gravity falls to 1.010. Rack into 5 quart (4.5 liter) jars or a secondary fermentation vessel fitted with an airlock. Add gelatin before fitting airlocks.

6 Leave for 7 days before racking the beer from the sediment into a primed pressure barrel. Allow 7 days conditioning before sampling.

Pompey Royal

RECIPE BASED ON POMPEY ROYAL BY WHITBREAD (MADE BY GALE'S OF HORNDEAN).

Once Brickwoods Brewery's Best Bitter, this robust brew is good value for the money since you can still taste the hops hours after supping it—and there are not many brews that can boast such a strength of flavor.

Stage	25 quarts	Original gravity 1.047	25 liters
1	5½ lb.	Crushed pale malt	2800 gm
1	8 oz.	Crushed crystal malt	250 gm
1	15 quarts	Water for bitter brewing	15 liters
3	1 tsp.	Irish moss	5 ml
3	1 lb.	Barley syrup	500 gm
3	1 lb.	Dark brown sugar	500 gm
3	2 oz.	Fuggles hops	60 gm
3	1 oz.	Bramling cross hops	30 gm
3, 4	(½ + ½) oz.	Goldings hops	(15 + 15) gm
5	2 oz.	Brewer's yeast	60 gm
5	½ oz.	Gelatin	15 gm
6	2 oz.	Brown sugar	60 gm

Brewing Stages

1 Raise the water temperature to 140°F (60°C). Stir in the crushed malts. Stirring continuously, raise the mash temperature to 151°F (66°C). Leave for 1½ hours, occasionally returning temperature back to this value.

2 Pour the mashed grain into a large grain bag and rinse with water slightly hotter than the mash to collect 20 quarts (19 liters) of extract.

3 Boil extract with the Fuggles and Bramling Cross hops and first quota of Goldings hops for 1½ hours. Dissolve the dark brown sugar and syrup in hot water and add during boil. Add the Irish moss as directed on the instructions.

4 Turn off the heat, stir in the second batch of Goldings hops and soak for 15 minutes. Strain the clear wort into a fermenting bucket and top up to final quantity with cold water.

5 Add yeast when cool to room temperature. Ferment 4–5 days until the specific gravity falls to 1.012. Rack into 5 quart (4.5 liter) jars or a 25 quart (24 liter) fermenter fitted with an airlock. Add gelatin before fitting airlocks.

6 Leave for 7 days before racking the beer from the sediment into a primed pressure barrel. Condition for 7 days before sampling.

Trophy

RECIPE BASED ON TROPHY BY WHITBREAD (FLOWERS, CHELTENHAM).

Trophy is a generic term for many of the best bitters under the Whitbread banner.

Stage	25 quarts	Original gravity 1.037	25 liters
1	4 lb.	Crushed pale malt	2000 gm
1	5 oz.	Flaked barley	150 gm
1	12.5 quarts	Water for bitter brewing	12 liters
3	1 tsp.	Irish moss	5 ml
3	1 lb.	Barley syrup	500 gm
3	1 lb.	Dark brown sugar	500 gm
3	2 oz.	Fuggles hops	60 gm
3, 4, 5	(1 + ¼ + ¼) oz.	Goldings hops	(30 + 10 + 10) gm
5	2 oz.	Brewer's yeast	60 gm
5	½ oz.	Gelatin	15 gm
6	2 oz.	Brown sugar	60 gm

Brewing Stages

1 Raise the water temperature to 140°F (60°C). Stir in the crushed malt and grain. Stirring continuously, raise the mash temperature to 151°F (66°F). Leave for 1½ hours, occasionally returning the temperature back to this value.

2 Pour the mashed grain into a large bag and rinse with water slightly hotter than the mash to collect 20 quarts (19 liters) of extract.

3 Boil the extract with the Fuggles hops and first quota of Goldings hops for 1½ hours. Dissolve the dark brown sugar and barley syrup in hot water and add during boil. Add Irish moss as directed on instructions.

4 Turn off heat, stir in second batch of Goldings hops, and allow to soak for 15 minutes. Strain the clear wort into a fermenting bucket and top up to the final quantity with cold water.

5 Add yeast when cool to room temperature. Ferment 4–5 days until the specific gravity falls to 1.010. Rack into 5 quart (4.5 liter) jars or a secondary fermentation vessel fitted with an airlock. Add gelatin and the remaining hops before fitting airlocks.

6 Leave 7 days before racking the beer from the sediment into a primed pressure barrel. Condition for 7 days before sampling.

Young's Special Bitter

RECIPE BASED ON SPECIAL BITTER BY YOUNG'S, WANDSWORTH.

A strong, hoppy bitter with a distinctive taste.

Stage	25 quarts	Original gravity 1.047	25 liters
1	7½ lb.	Crushed pale malt	3750 gm
1	5 oz.	Crushed crystal malt	150 gm
1	15 quarts	Water for bitter brewing	15 liters
3	1 tsp.	Irish moss	5 ml
3	2 oz.	Fuggles hops	60 gm
3, 4, 5	(1¼ + ½ + ¼) oz.	Goldings hops	(40 + 15 + 10) gm
3, 6	(12 + 2) oz.	Raw brown sugar	(400 + 60) gm
5	2 oz.	Brewer's yeast	60 gm
5	½ oz.	Gelatin	15 gm

125

Brewing Stages

1 Raise the temperature of the water to 140°F (60°C) and stir in the crushed malts. Stirring continuously, raise the mash temperature to 151°F (66°C). Leave for 1½ hours, occasionally returning the temperature back to this value.

2 Pour the mashed grain into a large grain bag to retrieve the sweet wort. Using water slightly hotter than the mash, rinse the grains to collect 20 quarts (19 liters) of extract.

3 Boil the extract with the Fuggles hops and the first quota of Goldings hops for 1½ hours. Dissolve the main batch of sugar in a little hot water and add this during the boil. Also add the Irish moss as directed on the instructions.

4 Turn off the heat, stir in the second batch of Goldings hops and allow them to soak for 15 minutes. Strain the clear wort into a fermenting bucket and top up to the final quantity with cold water.

5 When cool to room temperature, add the yeast. Ferment 4–5 days until the specific gravity falls to 1.012. Rack into 5 quart (4.5 liter) jars or a 25 quart (24 liter) fermenter fitted with an airlock. Add gelatin and the rest of the dry hops before fitting airlocks.

6 Leave for 7 days before racking the beer from the sediment into a primed pressure barrel. Allow 7 days conditioning before sampling.

CHAPTER 5

Keg Beers

Worthington E

RECIPE BASED ON WORTHINGTON E BY BASS.

Full, malty keg bitter with a very strong flavor of hops.

Stage	25 quarts	4% Alcohol	25 liters
1	4 lb.	Malt extract syrup	2000 gm
1	8 oz.	Crushed crystal malt	250 gm
1	1½ lb.	Brown sugar	750 gm
1	2 oz.	Fuggles hops	60 gm
1	10 quarts	Water for bitter brewing	10 liters
2	2 oz. (equiv.)	Hop extract	60 gm
2	1 oz.	Home brew beer yeast	30 gm
2	½ oz.	Gelatin	15 gm
3	2 oz.	White sugar	60 gm

Brewing Stages

1 Boil the malt extract, crushed malt and Fuggles hops in water for 45 minutes. Carefully strain the wort from the hops and malt grains into a fermenting bucket. Rinse the spent grains and hops with two pots of hot water. Dissolve the brown sugar in hot water and add this to the bucket. Top up to the final quantity with cold water.

2 When cool to room temperature, add the yeast and hop extract. Ferment 4–5 days until the activity abates. Rack into secondary fermentation vessels and keep under airlock protection for another 3 days. Add gelatin and keep the beer under airlock protection for another 7 days.

3 Rack the beer off the sediment into a primed beer barrel. Allow 7 days conditioning before sampling.

Draft John Courage

RECIPE BASED ON DRAUGHT JOHN COURAGE BY COURAGE.

Draft version of the bottled strong bitter. Smooth, sweet, mellow brew with a smack of hops.

Stage	25 quarts	Original gravity 1.045	25 liters
1	6½ lb.	Crushed pale malt	3250 gm
1	8 oz.	Torrefied barley	250 gm
1	4 oz.	Crushed crystal malt	125 gm
1	15 quarts	Water for bitter brewing	15 liters
3	1 tsp.	Irish moss	5 ml
3	1 lb.	Light brown sugar	500 gm
3	3 oz.	Goldings hops	100 gm
3	½ oz.	Northern Brewer hops	15 gm
5	2 oz.	Brewer's yeast	60 gm
5	½ oz.	Gelatin	15 gm
6	2 oz.	Brown sugar	60 gm

Brewing Stages

1 Raise the temperature of the water to 140°F (60°C) and stir in the crushed malts and torrefied barley. Stirring continuously, raise the mash temperature to 151°F (66°C). Leave for 1½ hours, occasionally returning the temperature back to this value.

2 Pour the mashed grain into a large grain bag to retrieve the sweet wort. Using water slightly hotter than the mash, rinse the grains to collect 20 quarts (19 liters) of extract.

3 Boil the extract with the hops for 1½ hours. Dissolve the light brown sugar in a little hot water and add this during the boil. Also add the Irish moss as directed on the instructions.

4 Turn off the heat, strain the clear wort into a fermenting bucket and top up to the final quantity with cold water.

5 When cool to room temperature, add the yeast. Ferment 4–5 days until the specific gravity falls to 1.012. Rack into 5 quart (4.5 liter) jars or a secondary fermentation vessel fitted with an airlock. Add gelatin before fitting airlocks.

6 Leave for 7 days before racking the beer from the sediment into a primed pressure barrel. Allow 7 days conditioning before sampling.

Tavern Keg

RECIPE BASED ON TAVERN KEG BY COURAGE.

Remarkable palate fullness. Malty and heavy with just enough hops.

Stage	25 quarts	Original gravity 1.039	25 liters
1	3 lb.	Diastatic malt extract	1500 gm
1	8 oz.	Flaked barley	250 gm
1	8 oz.	Crushed crystal malt	250 gm
1, 3	(1 lb. 14 oz. + 2 oz.)	Light brown sugar	(950 + 60) gm
1	2 oz.	Fuggles hops	60 gm
1	1 oz. (equiv.)	Hop extract	30 gm (equiv.)
1	12.5 quarts	Water for bitter brewing	12 liters
2	1 oz.	Home brewer's beer yeast	30 gm
2	½ oz.	Gelatin	15 gm

Brewing Stages

1 Stir the malt and malt extract, Fuggles hops, hop extract, and barley in lukewarm water. Slowly raise to boiling point over 30 minutes, and then boil for 45 minutes. Carefully strain the wort from the hops and malt grains into a fermenting bucket. Rinse the spent grains and hops with two pots of hot water. Dissolve the main batch of sugar in hot water and add this to the bucket. Top up to the final quantity with cold water.

2 When cool to room temperature, add the yeast. Ferment 4–5 days until the activity abates. Rack into secondary fermentation vessels and keep under airlock protection for another 3 days. Add gelatin and keep the beer under airlock protection for another 5 days.

3 Rack the beer off the sediment into a primed beer barrel. Allow 3 days conditioning before sampling.

Double Diamond

RECIPE BASED ON DOUBLE DIAMOND BY IND, COOPE & CO. (CARLSBERG-TETLEY), BURTON-ON-TRENT.

Popular keg bitter reputed to work wonders for its loyal following. Until starting on this book, I could not recollect how it tasted. Now that I have supped and brewed some, it rates as one of the best keg bitters.

Stage	25 quarts	Original gravity 1.038	25 liters
1	5½ lb.	Crushed pale malt	2800 gm
1	12.5 quarts	Water for bitter brewing	12 liters
3	1 lb.	Barley syrup	500 gm
3	5	Saccharin tablets	5
3	2 oz.	Fuggles hops	60 gm
3	1 tsp.	Irish moss	5 ml
3, 6	(6 + 2) oz.	Dark brown sugar	(200 + 60) gm
5	2 oz. (equiv.)	Hop extract	60 gm (equiv.)
5	2 oz.	Brewer's yeast	60 gm
5	½ oz.	Gelatin	15 gm

Brewing Stages

1 Raise the temperature of the water to 140°F (60°C) and stir in the crushed malt. Stirring continuously, raise the mash temperature to 151°F (66°C). Leave for 1½ hours, occasionally returning the temperature back to this value.

2 Pour the mashed grain into a large grain bag to retrieve the sweet wort. Using water slightly hotter than the mash, rinse the grains to collect 20 quarts (19 liters) of extract.

3 Boil the extract with the Fuggles hops for 1½ hours. Dissolve the main batch of sugar, saccharin and syrup in a little hot water and add this during the boil. Also add the Irish moss as directed on the instructions.

4 Turn off the heat, strain the clear wort into a fermenting bucket and top up to the final quantity with cold water.

5 When cool to room temperature, add the yeast and hop extract, Ferment 4–5 days until the specific gravity falls to 1.010. Rack into 5 quart (4.5 liter) jars or a 25 quart (24 liter) fermenter fitted with an airlock. Add gelatin before fitting airlocks.

6 Leave for 7 days before racking the beer from the sediment into a primed pressure barrel. Allow 7 days conditioning before sampling.

Yorkshire Bitter

RECIPE BASED ON YORKSHIRE BITTER BY JOHN SMITH'S, TADCASTER.

Pleasant keg bitter with a good head retention and nice amber color. Satisfying hop flavor.

Stage	25 quarts	Original gravity 1.037	25 liters
1	3 lb.	Crushed pale malt	1500 gm
1	2 oz.	Crushed wheat malt	60 gm
1	10 quarts	Water for bitter brewing	10 liters
3	1 tsp.	Irish moss	5 ml
3	2 lb.	Diastatic malt extract	1000 gm
3	1 oz.	Bramling Cross hops	30 gm
3, 4	(1½ + ½) oz.	Goldings hops	(45 + 10) gm
3, 6	(14 + 2) oz.	Dark brown sugar	(450 + 50) gm
5	2 oz.	Brewer's yeast	60 gm
5	½ oz.	Gelatin	15 gm

Brewing Stages

1 Raise the temperature of the water to 140°F (60°C) and stir in the crushed malts. Stirring continuously, raise the temperature to 151°F (66°C). Leave for 1½ hours, occasionally returning the temperature back to this value.

2 Pour the mashed grain into a large grain bag to retrieve the sweet wort. Using water slightly hotter than the mash, rinse the grains to collect 15 quarts (14 liters) of extract.

3 Boil the extract with the Bramling Cross hops and the first quota of Goldings hops for 1½ hours. Dissolve the main batch of sugar and malt extract in hot water and add this during the boil. Also add the Irish moss as directed on the instructions.

4 Turn off the heat, stir in the second batch of Goldings hops and allow them to soak for 15 minutes. Strain the clear wort into a fermenting bucket and top up to the final quantity with cold water.

5 When cool to room temperature, add the yeast. Ferment 4–5 days until the specific gravity falls to 1.010. Rack into 5 quart (4.5 liter) jars or a secondary fermentation vessel fitted with an airlock. Add gelatin before fitting airlocks.

6 Leave for 7 days before racking the beer from the sediment into a primed pressure barrel. Allow 7 days conditioning before sampling.

Ben Truman's Export

RECIPE BASED ON BEN TRUMAN'S EXPORT BY TRUMAN.

Popular keg beer with a nice yeasty, sweet bouquet.

Stage	25 quarts	Original gravity 1.036	25 liters
1	4 lb.	Crushed pale malt	2000 gm
1	4 oz.	Crushed wheat malt	125 gm
1	1 lb.	Flaked corn	500 gm
1	12.5 quarts	Water for bitter brewing	12 liters
3	1 tsp.	Irish moss	5 ml
3	1 lb.	Light brown sugar	500 gm
3	2 oz.	Fuggles hops	60 gm
5	1 oz. (equiv.)	Hop extract	30 gm (equiv.)
5	2 oz.	Brewer's yeast	60 gm
5	½ oz.	Gelatin	15 gm
6	2 oz.	White sugar	60 gm

131

Brewing Stages

1 Raise the temperature of the water to 140°F (60°C) and stir in the crushed malts and flaked corn. Stirring continuously, raise the mash temperature to 151°F (66°C). Leave for 1½ hours, occasionally returning the temperature back to this value.

2 Pour the mashed grain into a large grain bag to retrieve the sweet wort. Using water slightly hotter than the mash, rinse the grains to collect 20 quarts (19 liters) of extract.

3 Boil the extract with the Fuggles hops for 1½ hours. Dissolve the light brown sugar in a little hot water and add this during the boil. Also add the Irish moss as directed on the instructions.

4 Turn off the heat, strain the clear wort into a fermenting bucket and top up to the final quantity with cold water.

5 When cool to room temperature, add the yeast and hop extract. Ferment 4–5 days until the specific gravity falls to 1.010. Rack into 5 quart (4.5 liter) jars or a 25 quart (4.5 liter) fermenter fitted with an airlock. Add gelatin before fitting airlocks.

6 Leave for 7 days before racking the beer from the sediment into a primed pressure barrel. Allow 7 days conditioning before sampling.

Watney Mann Special Bitter

RECIPE BASED ON SPECIAL BITTER BY WATNEY MANN.

Best selling keg bitter.

Stage	25 quarts	3.5% Alcohol	25 liters
1	2 lb.	Malt extract syrup	1000 gm
1	4 oz.	Crushed crystal malt	125 gm
1	8 oz.	Brewing sugar	250 gm
1	2 lb.	Raw brown sugar	1000 gm
1	1 oz.	Fuggles hops	30 gm
1	12.5 quarts	Water for bitter brewing	12 liters
1	1 tsp.	Irish moss	5 ml
2	½ oz.	Gelatin	15 gm
2	1 oz.	Home brew beer yeast	30 gm
2	1 oz. (equiv.)	Hop extract	30 gm (equiv.)
2	4	Saccharin tablets	4
3	2 oz.	White sugar	60 gm

Brewing Stages

1 Boil the malt extract, Irish moss, Fuggles hops and crystal malt in water for 45 minutes. Carefully strain the wort from the hops and malt grains into a fermenting bucket. Rinse the spent grains and hops with two pots of hot water. Dissolve the brewing sugar and brown sugar in hot water and add this to the bucket. Top up to the final quantity with cold water.

2 When cool to room temperature, add the yeast, saccharin tablets and hop extract. Ferment 4–5 days until the activity abates. Rack into secondary fermentation vessels and keep under airlock protection for another 7 days. Add gelatin and keep the beer under airlock protection for another 7 days.

3 Rack the beer off the sediment into a primed beer barrel. Allow 3 days conditioning before sampling.

Starlight Bitter

RECIPE BASED ON STARLIGHT BITTER BY WATNEY MANN.

Well-balanced, light gravity keg bitter.

Stage	25 quarts	Original gravity 1.032	25 liters
1	4 lb.	Crushed pale malt	2000 gm
1	8 oz.	Flaked corn	250 gm
1	4 oz.	Flaked barley	125 gm
1	12.5 quarts	Water for bitter brewing	12 liters
3	1 tsp.	Irish moss	5 ml
3	1 lb.	Brewing sugar	500 gm
3	1 oz.	Fuggles hops	30 gm
5	1 oz. (equiv.)	Hop extract	30 gm (equiv.)
5	2 oz.	Brewer's yeast	60 gm
5	½ oz.	Gelatin	15 gm
6	2 oz.	White sugar	60 gm

133

Brewing Stages

1 Raise the temperature of the water to 140°F (60°C) and stir in the crushed malt, and flaked corn and barley. Stirring continuously, raise the mash temperature to 151°F (66°C) Leave for 1½ hours, occasionally returning the temperature back to this value.

2 Pour the mashed grain into a large grain bag to retrieve the sweet wort. Using water slightly hotter than the mash, rinse the grains to collect 20 quarts (19 liters) of extract.

3 Boil the extract with the Fuggles hops for 1½ hours. Dissolve the brewing sugar in a little hot water and add this during the boil. Also add the Irish moss as directed on the instructions.

4 Strain the clear wort into a fermenting bucket and top up to the final quantity with cold water.

5 When cool to room temperature, add the yeast and hop extract. Ferment 4–5 days until the specific gravity falls to 1.010. Rack into 5 quart (4.5 liter) jars or a secondary fermentation vessel fitted with an airlock. Add gelatin before fitting airlocks.

6 Leave for 7 days before racking the beer from the sediment into a primed pressure barrel. Allow 3 days conditioning before sampling.

Special Mild

RECIPE BASED ON SPECIAL MILD BY WATNEY MANN.

Watney always had a good name for brewing dark beers and this popular brew was better than the majority of mild ales I sampled. Judging by the number of people who drank it, others felt the same way.

Stage	25 quarts	Original gravity 1.031	25 liters
1	4¼ lb.	Crushed pale malt	2200 gm
1	4 oz.	Flaked barley	125 gm
1	12.5 quarts	Water for mild ale brewing	12 liters
3	1 lb.	Dark brown sugar	500 gm
3	2 oz.	Black treacle	60 gm
3	1 oz.	Fuggles hops	30 gm
5	5	Saccharin tablets	5
5	1½ oz. (equiv.)	Hop extract	50 gm (equiv.)
5	2 oz.	Brewer's yeast	60 gm
5	½ oz.	Gelatin	15 gm
6	2 oz.	Brown sugar	60 gm

Brewing Stages

1 Raise the temperature of the water to 140°F (60°C) and stir in the crushed malt and flaked barley. Stirring continuously, raise the mash temperature to 151°F (66°C). Leave for 1½ hours, occasionally returning the temperature back to this value.

2 Pour the mashed grain into a large grain bag to retrieve the sweet wort. Using water slightly hotter than the mash, rinse the grains to collect 20 quarts (19 liters) of extract.

3 Boil the extract with the Fuggles hops for 1½ hours. Dissolve the dark brown sugar and black treacle in a little hot water and add this during the boil.

4 Turn off the heat, strain the clear wort into a fermenting bucket and top up to the final quantity with cold water.

5 When cool to room temperature, add the yeast, hop extract and saccharin tablets. Ferment 4–5 days until the specific gravity falls to 1.010. Rack into 5 quart (4.5 liter) jars or a 25 quart (24 liter) fermenter fitted with an airlock. Add gelatin before fitting airlocks.

6 Leave for 7 days before racking the beer from the sediment into a primed pressure barrel. Allow 5 days conditioning before sampling.

Tankard

RECIPE BASED ON TANKARD BY WHITBREAD.

Full-bodied keg bitter with well-balanced smooth flavor.

Stage	25 quarts	Original gravity 1.039	25 liters
1	4½ lb.	Crushed pale malt	2250 gm
1	4 oz.	Crushed torrefied barley	125 gm
1	15 quarts	Water for bitter brewing	15 liters
3	1 lb.	Barley syrup	500 gm
3	1 tsp.	Irish moss	5 ml
3	2 oz.	Fuggles hops	60 gm
3, 4	(1 + ½) oz.	Bramling Cross hops	(30 + 15) gm
3, 6	(14 + 2) oz.	Raw brown sugar	(450 + 50) gm
5	2 oz.	Brewer's yeast	60 gm
5	½ oz.	Gelatin	15 gm

Brewing Stages

1 Raise the temperature of the water to 140°F (60°C) and stir in the crushed malt and barley. Stirring continuously, raise the mash temperature to 151°F (66°C). Leave for 1½ hours, occasionally returning the temperature back to this value.

2 Pour the mashed grain into a large bag to retrieve the sweet wort. Using water slightly hotter than the mash, rinse the grains to collect 20 quarts (19 liters) of extract.

3 Boil the extract with the Fuggles hops and the first quota of Bramling Cross hops for 1½ hours. Dissolve the main batch of sugar and syrup in a little hot water and add this during the boil. Also add the Irish moss as directed on the instructions.

4 Turn off the heat, stir in the second batch of Bramling Cross hops and allow them to soak for 15 minutes. Strain the clear wort into a fermenting bucket and top up to the final quantity with cold water.

5 When cool to room temperature, add the yeast. Ferment 4–5 days until the specific gravity falls to 1.010. Rack into 5 quart (4.5 liter) jars or a secondary fermentation vessel fitted with an airlock. Add gelatin before fitting airlocks.

6 Leave for 7 days before racking the beer from the sediment into a primed pressure barrel. Allow 7 days conditioning before sampling.

Tartan Keg

RECIPE BASED ON TARTAN KEG BY YOUNGER, EDINBURGH.

A predominant hop flavor is the main characteristic of this malty keg bitter.
A relatively low carbonation makes it a smooth drink.

Stage	25 quarts	Original gravity 1.036	25 liters
1	4½ lb.	Crushed pale malt	2250 gm
1	4 oz.	Crushed flaked barley	125 gm
1	12.5 quarts	Water for pale ale brewing	12 liters
3	1 tsp.	Irish moss	5 ml
3	1 lb.	Malt extract syrup	500 gm
3	½ lb.	Dark brown sugar	250 gm
3	2 oz.	Fuggles hops	60 gm
3	1½ oz.	Northern Brewer hops	45 gm
5	2 oz.	Brewer's yeast	60 gm
5	½ oz.	Gelatin	15 gm
6	2 oz.	White sugar	60 gm

Brewing Stages

1 Raise the temperature of the water to 140°F (60°C) and stir in the crushed malt and flaked barley. Stirring continuously, raise the mash temperature to 151°F (66°C). Leave for 1½ hours, occasionally returning the temperature back to this value.

2 Pour the mashed grain into a large grain bag to retrieve the sweet wort. Using water slightly hotter than the mash, rinse the grains to collect 20 quarts (19 liters) of extract.

3 Boil the extract with the hops for 1½ hours. Dissolve the malt extract syrup and the dark brown sugar in a little hot water and add this during the boil. Also add the Irish moss as directed on the instructions.

4 Turn off the heat, strain the clear wort into a fermenting bucket and top up to the final quantity with cold water.

5 When cool to room temperature, add the yeast. Ferment 4–5 days until the specific gravity falls to 1.010. Rack into 5 quart (4.5 liter) jars or a 25 quart (24 liter) fermenter fitted with an airlock. Add gelatin before fitting airlocks.

6 Leave for 7 days before racking the beer from the sediment into a primed pressure barrel. Allow 7 days conditioning before sampling.

Beers of the World

Castlemaine XXXX Bitter

Not like a traditional English bitter beer but more of a hoppy lager. Nevertheless, a very palatable and refreshing brew.

Stage	25 quarts	Original gravity 1.044	25 liters
1	5¾ lb.	Crushed pale malt	2900 gm
1	1 lb.	Flaked corn	500 gm
1	15 quarts	Water for lager brewing	15 liters
3	1 tsp.	Irish moss	5 ml
3	1 lb.	Brewing sugar	500 gm
3	2¾ oz.	Hallertau hops	80 gm
5	2 oz.	Lager yeast	60 gm
5	½ oz.	Gelatin	15 gm
6	½ tsp./20 fl. oz.	White sugar	5 ml/liter

Brewing Stages

1 Raise water temperature to 131°F (55°C). Stir in crushed malt and flaked corn. Stirring constantly, raise temperature to 151°F (66°C). Leave for 1½ hours, occasionally returning the temperature back to this value.

2 Pour the mashed grain into a large grain bag and rinse with water slightly hotter than the mash to collect 20 quarts (19 liters) or extract.

3 Boil the extract and hops for 1½ hours. Dissolve the brewing sugar in hot water and add during the boil. Add the Irish moss as directed on the instructions.

4 Turn off the heat, strain the clear wort into a fermenting bucket, and top up to the final quantity with cold water.

5 Add the yeast when cool to room temperature. Ferment 4–5 days until the specific gravity falls to 1.012 and rack. Add gelatin before fitting airlocks.

6 Leave for 7 days before racking the beer from the sediment into primed beer bottles. Mature for 7 days before sampling.

Foster's Lager

This famous brew has a delicate flavor with a beery bouquet. Serve well chilled.

Stage	25 quarts	Original gravity 1.046	25 liters
1	6½ lb.	Crushed lager malt	3250 gm
1	1 lb.	Flaked rice	500 gm
1	15 quarts	Water for lager brewing	15 liters
3	1 tsp.	Irish moss	5 ml
3	12 oz.	Brewing sugar	400 gm
3	1½ oz.	Hallertau hops	45 gm
5	2 oz.	Lager yeast	60 gm
5	½ oz.	Gelatin	15 gm
6	½ tsp./20 fl. oz.	White sugar	5 ml/liter

Brewing Stages

1 Raise the temperature of the water to 113°F (45°C) and stir in the crushed malt and flaked rice. Stirring continuously, raise the mash temperature to 131°F (55°C). Let it stand for half an hour and then raise the temperature again to 151°F (66°C). Leave for 1½ hours, occasionally returning the temperature back to this value.

2 Pour the mashed grain into a large grain bag to retrieve the sweet wort. Using water slightly hotter than the mash, rinse the grains to collect 20 quarts (19 liters) of extract.

3 Boil the extract with the hops for 1½ hours. Dissolve the brewing sugar in a little hot water and add this during the boil. Also add the Irish moss as directed on the instructions.

4 Turn off the heat, strain the clear wort into a fermenting bucket and top up to the final quantity with cold water.

5 When cool to room temperature, add the yeast. Ferment in a cool place until the specific gravity falls to 1.012. Rack into 5 quart (4.5 liter) jars or a secondary fermentation vessel fitted with an airlock. Add gelatin before fitting airlocks.

6 Leave for 14 days before racking the beer from the sediment into primed beer bottles. Allow 21 days maturation before sampling.

Resch's Pilsner

Brewed and canned by Tooth and Co., this lager has ample strength and flavor despite the relatively low hop rate.

Stage	25 quarts	Original gravity 1.043	25 liters
1	5 lb.	Crushed lager malt	2500 gm
1	½ lb.	Flaked corn	250 gm
1	15 quarts	Water for lager brewing	15 liters
3	1 tsp.	Irish moss	5 ml
3	2 lb.	Cane syrup	1000 gm
3	1½ oz.	Hallertau hops	50 gm
5	2 oz.	Lager yeast	60 gm
5	½ oz.	Gelatin	15 gm
6	2 oz.	White sugar	60 gm

Brewing Stages

1 Raise the temperature of the water to 113°F (45°C) and stir in the crushed malt and flaked corn. Stirring continuously, raise the mash temperature to 131°F (55°C). Let it stand for half an hour and then raise the temperature again to 151°F (66°C). Leave for 1½ hours, occasionally returning the temperature back to this value.

2 Pour the mashed grain into a large grain bag to retrieve the sweet wort. Using water slightly hotter than the mash, rinse the grains to collect 20 quarts (19 liters) of extract.

3 Boil the extract with the hops for 1½ hours. Dissolve the syrup in a little hot water and add this during the boil. Also add the Irish moss as directed on the instructions.

4 Turn off the heat, strain the clear wort into a fermenting bucket and top up to the final quantity with cold water.

5 When cool to room temperature, add the yeast. Ferment in a cool place until the specific gravity falls to 1.010. Rack into 5 quart (4.5 liter) jars or a 25 quart (24 liter) fermenter fitted with an airlock. Add gelatin before fitting airlocks.

6 Leave for 21 days before racking the beer from the sediment into primed beer bottles. Allow 21 days maturation before sampling.

Southwark Bitter

Light-flavored sweetish beer very much like a lager. Brewed by the Southern Australian Brewing Company in Adelaide.

Stage	25 quarts	Original gravity 1.041	25 liters
1	5¼ lb.	Crushed pale malt	2650 gm
1	1 lb.	Flaked corn	500 gm
1	15 quarts	Water for lager brewing	15 liters
3	1 tsp.	Irish moss	5 ml
3	12 oz.	Brewing sugar	400 gm
3	2½ oz.	Goldings hops	75 gm
5	5	Saccharin tablets	5
5	2 oz.	Lager yeast	60 gm
5	½ oz.	Gelatin	15 gm
6	½ tsp./20 fl. oz.	White sugar	5 ml/liter

Brewing Stages

1 Raise the temperature of the water to 131°F (55°C) and stir in the crushed malt and flaked corn. Stirring continuously, raise the mash temperature to 151°F (66°C). Leave for 1½ hours, occasionally returning the temperature back to this value.

2 Pour the mashed grain into a large grain bag to retrieve the sweet wort. Using water slightly hotter than the mash, rinse the grains to collect 20 quarts (19 liters) of extract.

3 Boil the extract with the hops for 1½ hours. Dissolve the brewing sugar in a little hot water and add this during the boil. Also add the Irish moss as directed on the instructions.

4 Turn off the heat, strain the clear wort into a fermenting bucket and top up to the final quantity with cold water.

5 When cool to room temperature, add the yeast and saccharin tablets. Ferment 4–5 days until the specific gravity falls to 1.012. Rack into 5 quart (4.5 liter) jars or a secondary fermentation vessel fitted with an airlock. Add gelatin before fitting airlocks.

6 Leave for 7 days before racking the beer from the sediment into primed beer bottles. Allow 7 days maturation before sampling.

Chimay

An outstanding naturally conditioned beer brewed by the Trappist monks in Chimay. They certainly know their business.

Deliciously smooth, sweet and mellow, it must rank as one of the best beers in the world. *Bon sante!*

Stage	15 quarts	Original gravity 1.075	15 liters
1	6½ lb.	Crushed pale malt	3250 gm
1	1 oz.	Crushed black malt	30 gm
1	15 quarts	Water for strong ale brewing	15 liters
3	12 oz.	Dark brown sugar	400 gm
3	8 oz.	Blended honey	250 gm
3	2 oz.	Hallertau hops	60 gm
3	1 oz.	Goldings hops	30 gm
4	2 oz.	Brewer's yeast	60 gm
6	½ tsp./20 fl. oz.	White sugar	5 ml/liter

Brewing Stages

1 Raise the temperature of the water to 131°F (55°C) and stir in the crushed malts. Stirring continuously raise the temperature to 151°F (66°C). Leave for 1½ hours, occasionally returning the temperature back to this value.

2 Pour the mashed grain into a large grain bag to retrieve the sweet wort. Using water slightly hotter than the mash, slowly and gently rinse the grains to collect 17.25 quarts (16 liters) of extract.

3 Dissolve the sugar and honey in a little water. Add to extract, along with hops, and boil until the volume has been reduced to just over 15 quarts (14 liters). Strain and divide equally among four 5 quart (4.5 liter) jars. Fit airlocks.

4 When cool, add the yeast and ferment until the vigorous activity abates. Siphon into three 5 quart (4.5 liter) jars, filling each to the base of the neck. Refit airlocks and check regularly to ensure they don't dry out.

5 It will take weeks to complete the fermentation, after which the beer should be racked again, taking with it a minute quantity of the yeast sediment.

6 Store for six months before bottling in primed beer bottles (preferably 7 fl. oz. [207 ml] bottles).

7 Mature for 18 months before sampling.

Stella Artois

Strong, beautifully brewed lager with a generous hop quota that rounds off the residual malt sweetness.

Stage	20 quarts	Original gravity 1.050	20 liters
1	7 lb.	Crushed lager malt	3500 gm
1	12 oz.	Crushed wheat malt	400 gm
	15 quarts	Water for lager brewing	15 liters
	1 tsp.	Irish moss	5 ml
13	1 ½ oz.	Hallertau hops	45 gm
33, 4	(1 ½ + ½) oz.	Saaz hops	(45 + 15) gm
5	2 oz.	Lager yeast	60 gm
5	½ oz.	Gelatin	15 gm
6	½ tsp./20 fl. oz.	White sugar	5 ml/liter

Brewing Stages

1 Raise the temperature of the water to 113°F (45°C) and stir in the crushed malts. Stirring continuously, raise the mash temperature to 131°F (55°C). Let it stand for half an hour and then raise the temperature again to 151°F (66°C). Leave for 1 ½ hours, occasionally returning the temperature back to this value.

2 Pour the mashed grain into a large grain bag to retrieve the sweet wort. Using water slightly hotter than the mash, rinse the grains to collect 20 quarts (19 liters) of extract.

3 Boil the extract with the Hallertau hops and the first quota of Saaz hops for 1 ½ hours. Add the Irish moss as directed on the instructions.

4 Turn off the heat, stir in the second batch of Saaz hops and allow them to soak for 15 minutes. Strain the clear wort into a fermenting bucket and top up to the final quantity with cold water.

5 When cool to room temperature, add the yeast. Ferment in a cool place until the specific gravity falls to 1.012. Rack into 5 quart (4.5 liter) jars or a 25 quart (24 liter) fermenter fitted with an airlock. Add gelatin before fitting airlocks.

6 Leave for 21 days before racking the beer from the sediment into primed beer bottles. Allow 21 days maturation before sampling.

CZECH REPUBLIC

Pilsner Urquell

Really called Pizenske Prazdo, it is sold as Pilsner Urquell, and it is from this German version that the word "pilsner" originated. One of the finest lagers in the world, with a tremendous depth of flavor from the malt and Saaz hops.

Stage	20 quarts	Original gravity 1.050	20 liters
1	7 lb. 10 oz.	Crushed lager malt	3850 gm
1	15 quarts	Water for lager brewing	15 liters
3	1 tsp.	Irish moss	5 ml
3, 4, 5	(2½ + ½ + ¼) oz.	Saaz hops	(75 + 15 + 10) gm
5	2 oz.	Lager yeast	60 gm
5	½ oz.	Gelatin	15 gm
6	½ tsp./20 fl. oz.	White sugar	5 ml/liter

Brewing Stages

1 Raise the temperature of the water to 113°F (45°C) and stir in the crushed malt. Stirring continuously, raise the mash temperature to 131°F (55°C). Let it stand for half an hour and then raise the temperature again to 151°F (66°C). Leave for 1 hour, occasionally returning the temperature back to this value.

2 Pour the mashed grain into a large grain bag to retrieve the sweet wort. Using water slightly hotter than the mash, rinse the grains to collect 20 quarts (19 liters) of extract.

3 Boil the extract with the first quota of hops for 1½ hours. Add the Irish moss as directed on the instructions.

4 Turn off the heat, stir in the second batch of hops and allow them to soak for 15 minutes. Strain the clear wort into a fermenting bucket and top up to the final quantity with cold water.

5 When cool to room temperature, add the yeast. Ferment in a cool place until the specific gravity falls to 1.015. Rack into 5 quart (4.5 liter) jars or a secondary fermentation vessel fitted with an airlock. Add gelatin and the rest of the dry hops before fitting airlocks.

6 Leave for 21 days before racking the beer from the sediment into primed beer bottles. Allow 30 days maturation before sampling.

FRANCE

Kronenbourg Export Lager

Enjoyable lager with a distinctive flavor.

Stage	25 quarts	Original gravity 1.052	25 liters
1	7 lb.	Crushed lager malt	3600 gm
1	1¼ lb.	Flaked corn	625 gm
1	15 quarts	Water for lager brewing	15 liters
3	1 tsp.	Irish moss	5 ml
3	1 lb.	Blended honey	500 gm
3	1 oz.	Goldings hops	30 gm
3, 4	(1¼+ ¼) oz.	Saaz hops	(40 + 10) gm
5	2 oz.	Lager yeast	60 gm
5	½ oz.	Gelatin	15 gm
6	½ tsp./20 fl. oz.	White sugar	5 ml/liter

Brewing Stages

1 Raise the temperature of the water to 113°F (45°C) and stir in the crushed malt and flaked corn. Stirring continuously, raise the mash temperature to 131°F (55°C). Let it stand for half an hour and then raise the temperature again to 151°F (66°C). Leave for 1½ hours, occasionally returning the temperature back to this value.

2 Pour the mashed grain into a large grain bag to retrieve the sweet wort. Using water slightly hotter than the mash, rinse the grains to collect 20 quarts (19 liters) of extract.

3 Boil the extract with the Goldings hops and first quota of Saaz hops for 1½ hours. Dissolve the honey in a little hot water and add this during the boil. Also add the Irish moss as directed on the instructions.

4 Turn off the heat, stir in the rest of the hops and allow them to soak for 15 minutes. Strain the clear wort into a fermenting bucket and top up to the final quantity with cold water.

5 When cool to room temperature, add the yeast. Ferment in a cool place until the specific gravity falls to 1.015. Rack into 5 quart (4.5 liter) jars or a secondary fermentation vessel fitted with an airlock. Add gelatin before fitting airlocks.

6 Leave for 30 days before racking the beer from the sediment into primed beer bottles. Allow 21 days conditioning before sampling.

GERMANY

Dortmunder Hansa Export

Full-bodied lager, slightly sweet with sufficient hop bite.

Stage	20 quarts	Original gravity 1.053	20 liters
1	8 lb.	Crushed lager malt	4000 gm
1	15 quarts	Water for lager brewing	15 liters
3	1 tsp.	Irish moss	5 ml
3	2½ oz.	Saaz hops	75 gm
5	2 oz.	Lager yeast	60 gm
5	½ oz.	Gelatin	15 gm
6	½ tsp./20 fl. oz.	White sugar	5 ml/liter

Brewing Stages

1 Raise the temperature of the water to 131°F (55°C) and stir in the crushed malt. Let it stand for half an hour and then raise the temperature again to 151°F (66°C). Leave for 1½ hours, occasionally returning the temperature back to this value.

2 Pour the mashed grain into a large grain bag to retrieve the sweet wort. Using water slightly hotter than the mash, rinse the grains to collect 20 quarts (19 liters) of extract.

3 Boil the extract with the hops for 1½ hours. Add the Irish moss as directed on the instructions.

4 Turn off the heat, strain the clear wort into a fermenting bucket and top up to the final quantity with cold water.

5 When cool to room temperature, add the yeast. Ferment in a cool place until the specific gravity falls to 1.015. Rack into 5 quart (4.5 liter) jars or a 25 quart (24 liter) fermenter fitted with an airlock. Add gelatin before fitting airlocks.

6 Leave for 21 days before racking the beer from the sediment into primed beer bottles. Allow 30 days maturation before sampling.

Holsten Pilsner Lager

A true German lager brewed and bottled in the country of origin following the *Reinheitsgebot* principles. (See the next recipe).

Stage	25 quarts	Original gravity 1.046	25 liters
1	8 1b.	Crushed lager malt	4000 gm
1	8 oz.	Crushed wheat malt	250 gm
1	5 oz.	Crushed crystal malt	150 gm
1	15 quarts	Water for lager brewing	15 liters
3	1 tsp.	Irish moss	5 ml
3	2¾ oz.	Hallertau hops	75 gm
4	½ oz.	Goldings hops	20 gm
5	2 oz.	Lager yeast	60 gm
5	½ oz.	Gelatin	15 gm
6	½ tsp./20 fl. oz.	White sugar	5 ml/liter

Brewing Stages

1 Raise the temperature of the water to 104°F (40°C) and stir in the crushed malts. Stirring continuously, raise the mash temperature to 122°F (50°C). Let it stand for half an hour and then raise the temperature again to 151°F (66°C). Leave for 1½ hours, occasionally returning the temperature back to this value.

2 Pour the mashed grain into a large grain bag to retrieve the sweet wort. Using water slightly hotter than the mash, rinse the grains to collect 20 quarts (19 liters) of extract.

3 Boil the extract with the Hallertau hops for 1½ hours. Add the Irish moss as directed on the instructions.

4 Turn off the heat, stir in the batch of Goldings hops and allow them to soak for 15 minutes. Strain the clear wort into a fermenting bucket and top up to the final quantity with cold water.

5 When cool to room temperature, add the yeast. Ferment in a cool place (50°F [10°C]) until the specific gravity falls to 1.012. Rack into 5 quart (4.5 liter) jars or a secondary fermentation vessel fitted with an airlock. Add gelatin before fitting airlocks.

6 Leave for 30 days before racking the beer from the sediment into primed beer bottles. Allow 30 days maturation before sampling.

Lowenbrau Light Blonde Special

In 1516, Duke Wilhelm IV of Bavaria decreed *Reinheitsgebot*, or "Pledge of Purity." According to this pledge, only barley hops and water should be used in the brewing of beer.

This strong, well-matured lager is an excellent example of beer brewed to the German Beer Purity standards.

Stage	20 quarts	Original gravity 1.060	20 liters
1	9 lb.	Crushed lager malt	4500 gm
1	3 oz.	Crushed crystal malt	100 gm
1	15 quarts	Water for lager brewing	15 liters
3	1 tsp.	Irish moss	5 ml
3	1 oz.	Hallertau hops	30 gm
3, 4, 5	(1½ + ¼ + ¼) oz.	Saaz hops	(45 + 10 + 10) gm
5	2 oz.	Lager yeast	60 gm
5	½ oz.	Gelatin	15 gm
6	½ tsp./20 fl. oz.	White sugar	5 ml/liter

Brewing stages

1 Raise the temperature of the water to 113°F (45°C) and stir in the crushed malts. Stirring continuously, raise the mash temperature to 131°F (55°C). Let it stand for half an hour and then raise the temperature again to 151°F (66°C). Leave for 1½ hours, occasionally returning the temperature back to this value.

2 Pour the mashed grain into a large grain bag to retrieve the sweet wort. Using water slightly hotter than the mash, rinse the grains to collect 20 quarts (19 liters) of extract.

3 Boil the extract with the Hallertau hops and the first quota of Saaz hops for 1½ hours. Add the Irish moss as directed on the instructions.

4 Turn off the heat, stir in the second batch of Saaz hops and allow them to soak for 15 minutes. Strain the clear wort into a fermenting bucket and top up to the final quantity with cold water.

5 When cool to room temperature, add the yeast. Ferment in a cool place until the specific gravity falls to 1.015. Rack into 5 quart (4.5 liter) jars or a 25 quart (24 liter) fermenter fitted with an airlock. Add gelatin and the rest of the dry hops before fitting airlocks.

6 Leave for 30 days before racking the beer from the sediment into primed beer bottles. Allow 30 days maturation before sampling.

ITALY

Peroni Birra

First class beer; certainly the best-looking lager I have come across.

Stage	25 quarts	Original gravity 1.044	25 liters
1	6½ lb.	Crushed lager malt	3250 gm
1	4 oz.	Crushed crystal malt	125 gm
1	1 lb. 8 oz.	Flaked rice	750 gm
1	15 quarts	Water for lager brewing	15 liters
3	1 tsp.	Irish moss	5 ml
3, 4	(2 + 1) oz.	Saaz hops	(60 + 30) gm
5	2 oz.	Lager yeast	60 gm
5	½ oz.	Gelatin	15 gm
6	½ tsp./20 fl. oz.	White sugar	5 ml/liter

Brewing Stages

1 Raise the temperature of the water to 113°F (45°C) and stir in the crushed malts and flaked rice. Stirring continuously, raise the mash temperature to 131°F (55°C). Let it stand for half an hour and then raise the temperature again to 151°F (66°C), Leave for one hour, occasionally returning the temperature back to this value.

2 Pour the mashed grain into a large grain bag to retrieve the sweet wort. Using water slightly hotter than the mash, rinse the grains to collect 20 quarts (19 liters) of extract.

3 Boil the extract with the first quota of Saaz hops for 1½ hours. Add the Irish moss as directed on the instructions.

4 Turn off the heat, stir in the second batch of hops and allow them to soak for 15 minutes. Strain the clear wort into a fermenting bucket and top up to the final quantity with cold water.

5 When cool to room temperature, add the yeast. Ferment in a cool place until the specific gravity falls to 1.012. Rack into 5 quart (4.5 liter) jars or a 25 quart (24 liter) fermenter fitted with an airlock. Add gelatin before fitting airlocks.

6 Leave for 21 days before racking the beer from the sediment into primed beer bottles. Allow 21 days conditioning before sampling.

LUXEMBOURG

Diekirch Lager

Typical high-class European lager. Everything is right about this brew—flavor, balance, color and strength—most enjoyable drink.

Stage	25 quarts	Original gravity 1.045	25 liters
1	8 lb.	Crushed lager malt	4000 gm
1	3 oz.	Crushed crystal malt	100 gm
1	15 quarts	Water for lager brewing	15 liters
3	1 tsp.	Irish moss	5 ml
3, 4	(2½ + ½) oz.	Saaz hops	(75 + 15) gm
5	2 oz.	Lager yeast	60 gm
5	½ oz.	Gelatin	15 gm
6	½ tsp./20 fl. oz.	White sugar	5 ml/liter

Brewing Stages

1 Raise the temperature of the water to 113°F (45°C) and stir in the crushed malts. Stirring continuously, raise the mash temperature to 131°F (55°C). Let it stand for half an hour and then raise the temperature again to 151°F (66°C). Leave for 1½ hours, occasionally returning the temperature back to this value.

2 Pour the mashed grain into a large grain bag to retrieve the sweet wort. Using water slightly hotter than the mash, rinse the grains to collect 20 quarts (19 liters) of extract.

3 Boil the extract with the first quota of hops for 1½ hours. Add the Irish moss as directed on the instructions.

4 Turn off the heat, stir in the second batch of hops and allow them to soak for 15 minutes. Strain the clear wort into a fermenting bucket and top up to the final quantity with cold water.

5 When cool to room temperature, add the yeast. Ferment in a cool place until the specific gravity falls to 1.012. Rack into 5 quart (4.5 liter) jars or a secondary fermentation vessel fitted with an airlock. Add gelatin before fitting airlocks.

6 Leave for 21 days before racking the beer from the sediment into primed beer bottles. Allow 24 days maturation before sampling.

THE NETHERLANDS

Grolsch Lager

From the Bierbrouwerij in Groenlo comes this very strong, full-flavored, completely natural lager.

Stage	15 quarts	Original gravity 1.068	15 liters
1	7½ lb.	Crushed lager malt	3750 gm
1	3 oz.	Crushed crystal malt	100 gm
1	15 quarts	Water for lager brewing	15 liters
3	1 tsp.	Irish moss	5 ml
3	3 oz.	Hallertau hops	100 gm
5	2 oz.	Lager yeast	60 gm
5	½ oz.	Gelatin	15 gm
6	½ tsp./20 fl. oz.	White sugar	5 ml/liter

Brewing Stages

1 Raise the temperature of the water to 113°F (45°C) and stir in the crushed malts. Stirring continuously, raise the mash temperature to 131°F (55°C). Let it stand for half an hour and then raise the temperature again to 151°F (66°C). Leave for 1½ hours, occasionally returning the temperature back to this value.

2 Pour the mashed grain into a large grain bag to retrieve the sweet wort. Using water slightly hotter than the mash, rinse the grains to collect 20 quarts (19 liters) of extract.

3 Boil the extract with the hops for 1½ hours. Add the Irish moss as directed on the instructions.

4 Turn off the heat, strain off the clear wort into a fermenting bucket and top up to the final quantity with cold water.

5 When cool to room temperature, add the yeast and ferment in a cool place for five days. Then rack into three 5 quart (4.5 liter) jars. Complete the fermentation. Rack into fresh jars and add gelatin before fitting airlocks again. Refit airlocks and check regularly to ensure they don't dry out.

6 Leave for 21 days before racking the beer from the sediment into primed beer bottles. Allow 30 days maturation before sampling.

POLAND

Zywiec Tatra

Pronounced "jeu-vee-etts tah-tra" if you are sober, but after a few glasses of this potent brew phrasing becomes a little difficult. I vaguely remember someone explaining it meant "mountain life" or "spirit" when translated. The hop flavor was excellent and the strength very adequate!

Stage	25 quarts	Original gravity 1.052	25 liters
1	6½ lb.	Crushed lager malt	3250 gm
1	8 oz.	Crushed wheat malt	250 gm
1	15 quarts	Water for lager brewing	15 liters
3	1 tsp.	Irish moss	5 ml
3	2 lb.	Cane syrup	1000 gm
3, 4	(2½ + ¼) oz.	Saaz hops	(75 + 10) gm
5	2 oz.	Lager yeast	60 gm
5	½ oz.	Gelatin	15 gm
6	½ tsp./20 fl. oz.	White sugar	5 ml/liter

Brewing Stages

1 Raise the temperature of the water to 113°F (45°C) and stir in the crushed malts. Stirring continuously, raise the mash temperature to 131°F (55°C). Let it stand for half an hour and then raise the temperature again to 151°F (66°C). Leave for 1½ hours, occasionally returning the temperature back to this value.

2 Pour the mashed grain into a large grain bag to retrieve the sweet wort. Using water slightly hotter than the mash, rinse the grains to collect 20 quarts (19 liters) of extract.

3 Boil the extract with the first quota of hops for 1½ hours. Dissolve the cane syrup in a little hot water and add this during the boil. Also add the Irish moss as directed on the instructions.

4 Turn off the heat, stir in the second batch of hops and allow them to soak for 15 minutes. Strain the clear wort into a fermenting bucket and top up to the final quantity with cold water.

5 When cool to room temperature, add the yeast. Ferment in a cool place until the specific gravity falls to 1.015. Rack into 5 quart (4.5 liter) jars or a 25 quart (24 liter) fermenter fitted with an airlock. Add gelatin before fitting airlocks.

6 Leave for 21 days before racking the beer from the sediment into primed beer bottles. Allow 21 days conditioning before sampling.

SINGAPORE

Tiger Lager

The first name in beer for people, especially those in the armed forces, who have visited the Eastern Countries. A light lager, but sweeter than most others for the gravity.

Stage	25 quarts	Original gravity 1.035	25 liters
1	5 lb.	Crushed lager malt	2500 gm
1	1 lb. 6 oz.	Flaked rice	650 gm
1	12.5 quarts	Water for lager brewing	12 liters
3	1 tsp.	Irish moss	5 ml
3	2 oz.	Hallertau hops	60 gm
5	10	Saccharin tablets	10
5	1 oz.	Lager yeast	60 gm
5	½ oz.	Gelatin	15 gm
6	½ tsp./20 fl. oz.	White sugar	5 ml/liter

Brewing Stages

1. Raise the temperature of the water to 113°F (45°C) and stir in the crushed malt and flaked rice. Stirring continuously, raise the mash temperature to 131°F (55°C). Let it stand for half an hour and then raise the temperature again to 151°F (66°C). Leave for 1½ hours, occasionally returning the temperature back to this value.

2. Pour the mashed grain into a large grain bag to retrieve the sweet wort. Using water slightly hotter than the mash, rinse the grains to collect 20 quarts (19 liters) of extract.

3. Boil the extract with the hops for 1½ hours. Also add the Irish moss as directed on the instructions.

4. Turn off the heat, strain the clear wort into a fermenting bucket and top up to the final quantity with cold water.

5. When cool to room temperature, add the yeast and saccharin tablets. Ferment in a cool place until the specific gravity falls to 1.008. Rack into 5 quart (4.5 liter) jars or a secondary fermentation vessel fitted with an airlock. Add gelatin before fitting airlocks.

6. Leave for 14 days before racking the beer from the sediment into primed beer bottles. Allow 21 days maturation before sampling.

SOUTH AFRICA

Castle Milk Stout

An excellent sweet stout brewed to a traditional-styled recipe for milk stouts.

Stage	20 quarts	Original gravity 1.037	20 liters
1	3½ lb.	Crushed pale malt	1750 gm
1	1 lb.	Flaked corn	500 gm
1	7 oz.	Crushed black malt	225 gm
1	12.5 quarts	Water for sweet stout brewing	12 liters
3	12 oz.	Light soft brown sugar	400 gm
3	2½ oz.	Saaz hops	75 gm
5	8 oz.	Lactose	250 gm
5	2 oz.	Brewer's yeast	60 gm
6	½ tsp./20 fl. oz.	White sugar	5 ml/liter

Brewing Stages

1 Raise the temperature of the water to 131°F (55°C) and stir in the crushed malt and flaked corn. Stirring continuously, raise the mash temperature to 151°F (66°C). Leave for 1½ hours, occasionally returning the temperature back to this value.

2 Pour the mashed grain into a large grain bag to retrieve the sweet wort. Using water slightly hotter than the mash, rinse the grains to collect 20 quarts (19 liters) of extract.

3 Boil the extract with the hops for 1½ hours. Dissolve the brown sugar in a little hot water and add this during the boil.

4 Turn off the heat, strain the clear wort into a fermenting bucket and top up to the final quantity with cold water.

5 When cool to room temperature, add the yeast. Dissolve lactose in a little water and add to mixture. Ferment 4–5 days until the specific gravity falls to 1.010. Rack into 5 quart (4.5 liter) jars or a 25 quart (24 liter) fermenter with an airlock, and fit airlocks.

6 Leave for 7 days before racking the beer from the sediment into primed beer bottles. Allow 10 days conditioning before sampling.

Lion Ale

A strong, sweet bitter brew with a lovely hop flavor.

Stage	25 quarts	Original gravity 1.046	25 liters
1	5 lb.	Crushed pale malt	2500 gm
1	1 lb. 5 oz.	Flaked corn	650 gm
1	15 quarts	Water for bitter brewing	15 liters
3	1 tsp.	Irish moss	5 ml
3	1 lb. 5 oz.	Brewing sugar	650 gm
3	2 tsp.	Brewer's caramel	10 ml
3	2 oz.	Saaz hops	60 gm
5	5	Saccharin tablets	5
5	2 oz.	Brewer's yeast	60 gm
5	½ oz.	Gelatin	15 gm
6	2 oz.	White sugar	60 gm

Brewing Stages

1 Raise the temperature of the water to 131°F (55°C) and stir in the crushed malt and flaked corn. Stirring continuously, raise the mash temperature to 151°F (66°C). Leave for 1½ hours, occasionally returning the temperature back to this value.

2 Pour the mashed grain into a large grain bag to retrieve the sweet wort. Using water slightly hotter than the mash, rinse the grains to collect 20 quarts (19 liters) of extract.

3 Boil the extract with the hops for 1½ hours. Dissolve the brewing sugar and the caramel in a little hot water and add this during the boil. Add the Irish moss as directed on the instructions.

4 Turn off the heat, strain the clear wort into a fermenting bucket and top up to the final quantity with cold water.

5 When cool to room temperature, add the yeast and saccharin tablets. Ferment 4–5 days until the specific gravity falls to 1.010. Rack into 5 quart (4.5 liter) jars or a secondary fermentation vessel fitted with an airlock. Add gelatin before fitting airlocks.

6 Leave for 7 days before racking the beer from the sediment into a primed pressure barrel. Allow 7 days conditioning before sampling.

SPAIN

San Miguel

Extremely good lager with a delicate, refreshing taste. Quite a strong brew.

Stage	20 quarts	5.5% Alcohol	20 liters
1	½ oz.	Hallertau hops	15 gm
1, 2	(80 + 160) fl. oz.	Water	(2 + 4) liters
2	4 lb. can	Home brew lager kit	1820 gm can
2	2 lb.	Cane syrup	1000 gm
2	½ oz.	Lager yeast	15 gm
4	½ tsp./20 fl. oz.	White sugar	5 ml/liter

Brewing Stages

1 Simmer the hops in water for ten minutes and strain off the liquid into a fermenting bucket.

2 Dissolve the lager kit contents and cane syrup in hot water and add this to the bucket as well. Top up to the final quantity with cold water and add the yeast.

3 Ferment until the gravity falls to 1.010. Rack into 5 quart (4.5 liter) jars or a 25 quart (24 liter) fermenter and fit airlock(s).

4 Leave for 7 days before bottling in primed beer bottles and mature for 14 days before sampling.

Hürlimann Sternbräu

Lightly flavored, sweet lager.

Stage	25 quarts	Original gravity 1.047	25 liters
1	6¼ lb.	Crushed lager malt	3175 gm
1	15 quarts	Water for lager brewing	15 liters
3	1 tsp.	Irish moss	5 ml
3	2 lb.	Cane syrup	1000 gm
3, 4	(1¾ + ¼) oz.	Saaz hops	(50 + 10) gm
5	5	Saccharin tablets	5
5	2 oz.	Lager yeast	60 gm
5	½ oz.	Gelatin	15 gm
6	½ tsp./20 fl. oz.	White sugar	5 ml/liter

Brewing Stages

1 Raise the temperature of the water to 113°F (45°C) and stir in the crushed malt. Stirring continuously, raise the mash temperature to 131°F (55°C). Let it stand for half an hour and then raise the temperature again to 151°F (66°C). Leave for one hour, occasionally returning the temperature back to this value.

2 Pour the mashed grain into a large grain bag to retrieve the sweet wort. Using water slightly hotter than the mash, rinse the grains to collect 20 quarts (19 liters) of extract.

3 Boil the extract with the first quota of Saaz hops for 1½ hours. Dissolve the syrup in a little hot water and add this during the boil. Also add the Irish moss as directed on the instructions.

4 Turn off the heat, stir in the second batch of hops and allow them to soak for 15 minutes. Strain the clear wort into a fermenting bucket and top up to the final quantity with cold water.

5 When cool to room temperature, add the yeast and saccharin tablets. Ferment in a cool place until the specific gravity falls to 1.012. Rack into 5 quart (4.5 liter) jars or a secondary fermentation vessel fitted with an airlock. Add gelatin before fitting airlocks.

6 Leave for 21 days before racking the beer from the sediment into the primed beer bottles. Allow 21 days maturation before sampling.

Index

Note: Page numbers in bold indicate recipe category lists. Page numbers in italics indicate recipes.

More Great Books from Fox Chapel Publishing

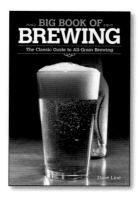

Big Book of Brewing
The Classic Guide to All-Grain Brewing
By Dave Line

Brewing your own beer is easier than you think with the easy-to-follow instructions in this book that teaches the simple "mashing" technique that produces the finest flavored beers, ales, stouts, and lagers.

ISBN: 978-1-56523-603-5
$17.95 · 256 Pages

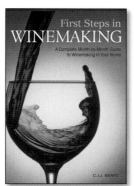

First Steps in Winemaking
A Complete Month-by-Month Guide to Winemaking in Your Home
By C. J. J. Berry

Delve into the world of at-home winemaking with methods and techniques that will turn your kitchen into a vineyard.

ISBN: 978-1-56523-602-8
$14.95 · 240 Pages

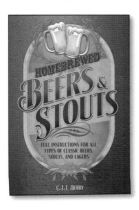

Homebrewed Beers & Stouts
Full Instructions for All Types of Classic Beers, Stouts, and Lagers
By C. J. J. Berry

Learn how to create light summer ales, pale lagers, or an authentic stout with over 70 recipes for brewing your own beer at home.

ISBN: 978-1-56523-601-1
$14.95 · 160 Pages

More Great Books from Fox Chapel Publishing

Real Cidermaking on a Small Scale
An Introduction to Producing Cider at Home
By Michael Pooley & John Lomax

Discover everything you need to know about making hard cider from any kind of apple—whether from your backyard or the local supermarket.

ISBN: 978-1-56523-604-2
$12.95 • 136 Pages

130 New Winemaking Recipes
Make Delicious Wine at Home Using Fruits, Grains, and Herbs
By C. J. J. Berry

Follow these 130 classic recipes for making wine in your own kitchen using traditional country ingredients.

ISBN: 978-1-56523-600-4
$12.95 • 136 Pages

Making Sparkling Wines at Home
By J. Restall and D. Hebbs

This book is focused on one subject—teaching readers how to make their own top-shelf sparkling wine.

ISBN: 978-1-56523-690-5
$12.95 • 120 Pages